Jennifer Pol Colin

PATTERNS

sew creative

13 Projects to Make Your Own • Tons of Techniques

FunStitch
STUDIO
an imprint of C&T Publishing

Publisher: Amy Marson	**Production Coordinator:** Tim Manibusan
Creative Director: Gailen Runge	**Production Editor:** Alice Mace Nakanishi
Editors: Karla Menaugh and Liz Aneloski	**Illustrator:** Linda Johnson
Technical Editor: Linda Johnson	**Photo Assistant:** Mai Yong Vang
Cover/Book Designer: April Mostek	**Photography** by Jennifer Pol Colin, unless otherwise noted

Published by FunStitch Studio, an imprint of C&T Publishing, Inc., P.O. Box 1456, Lafayette, CA 94549

Library of Congress Cataloging-in-Publication Data

Names: Colin, Jennifer Pol, 1979- author.

Title: Sew creative : 13 projects to make your own - tons of techniques / Jennifer Pol Colin.

Description: Lafayette, CA : C&T Publishing, Inc., 2018.

Identifiers: LCCN 2017045271 | ISBN 9781617456855 (soft cover)

Subjects: LCSH: Machine sewing.

Classification: LCC TT713 .C62 2018 | DDC 646.2/044--dc23

LC record available at https://lccn.loc.gov/2017045271

Printed in China

10 9 8 7 6 5 4 3 2 1

dedication

To Marlène, Louisa, and Marilou

acknowledgments

I feel so grateful for the people who have believed in me and supported me throughout my sewing journey.

First, I would like to thank my students. Without you, I wouldn't have learned how to sew and design so playfully. Many thanks are due to their parents who had confidence in me.

And because we all have to start somewhere, I will always feel very thankful for these people who gave me the first chance to teach what I love. Catherine and Gloria from the International School of Boston and Valérie from the San Diego French-American School, thank you.

Thank you to my friends, old and new, close and far, but most of all to my friend Barbara for supporting me when I opened my studio in San Diego; I didn't know a lot of people and I barely spoke English. Thanks to her daughter Ava too; I could not have hoped for a better student!

Of course, I would like to thank my dear family, who supports me all the time. First, to my husband and best friend, Olivier—thank you for being so positive, optimistic, and encouraging. Thank you for being who you are.

Thank you to my three sweet daughters—sewists and little artists who are so spontaneous and involved in my work. You are my muses, my models, and this entire book is designed for and with you!

Thank you, Mom, for your unfailing support of all my entrepreneurial endeavors. Thank you for truly believing in me. I love you.

Finally, thank you to my two grandmothers, who are both so talented and have such generous hearts. I always think of you in your sewing rooms as I'm sewing.

Thank you to all the contributors without whom the projects wouldn't look so nice: Dear Stella Fabrics, National Nonwovens, DMC Threads, and Coats & Clark. I appreciate the generous donations of great, high-quality fabrics and supplies.

Contents

 Beginner-friendly   *Some experience required*   *May I have some help, please?*

projects

Introduction

Sew Creative offers quick and simple projects, but also more sophisticated ones. You will find awesome projects for traveling, trendy clothing for everyday style, cool decor for your room, and useful accessories.

THIS BOOK IS DEFINITELY FOR YOU IF YOU ANSWER YES TO ANY OF THE FOLLOWING QUESTIONS:

Are you growing up and you want to affirm your own style?

Do you love to sew unique things and are you eager to discover new techniques?

Do you love arts and crafts?

Are you already a sewist with basic sewing skills?

If you have already gained confidence sewing by yourself this book is for you too!

You'll develop your sewing skills through very useful techniques and explore all the ways to personalize your sewing projects by using art supplies for modern sewists and crafters. Each project includes step-by-step instructions that are easy to follow as you create your own design.

For most of the projects, you have the choice of several designs so you can make a version that matches your personality. Look at the gallery photos at the end of each project to explore or find inspiration to create your very own version. If you want to make your project simple and plain—no worries; customization is just an option. But I will always encourage you to make your creation special and unique, because you are special and unique.

Are you ready to come along with me on a sewing journey?

Let's be creative and have fun!

—Jennifer

Fabrics and Supplies

get to know the fabrics

Most of the projects in this book are based on fabrics you could easily find in any fabric store. They are chosen for their neutral look, which makes them easy to customize.

Wovens

These come in millions of prints and solid colors and are made from threads going in two directions. The main direction is called the grainline or the length of grain, which is parallel to the selvage (the tightly woven edges where the manufacturer prints their brand name and the name of the designer). The other threads are woven crosswise, perpendicular to the selvage. Woven fabrics usually fray, so you may need to zigzag, baste or pink the edges.

QUILTING COTTON Quilting-quality cotton is light- or medium-weight and is easy to use and sew. It is available in a huge variety of prints, usually 42–44˝ wide.

DECORATOR-WEIGHT COTTON This cotton is much heavier than quilting cotton. Decorator cottons are usually 54˝ wide, which can be helpful for large projects. But the choice of prints is not as varied as quilting cotton, and the fabric can be a bit pricey.

CANVAS Unbleached cotton cloth (cotton canvas) is my favorite heavyweight fabric. It's ideal to paint on and use for lining. I love its neutral look. It comes in a 45˝ width and there is no real difference between the right or wrong side.

Knits

Although I use a nonstretchy sweater-knit fabric for the Dolman T-Shirt (page 63) and Raglan Sweatshirt (page 75), most knit fabrics are stretchy. Often, you have to use a zigzag stitch at the seams to keep the elasticity of the fiber. Before you cut any knit fabric, check to see which direction has the most stretch and make sure the length of the garment does not run parallel to this direction.

Felt

Felt is ideal for crafting and sewing; it's sturdy and its edges do not fray. Synthetic felt, which is made from recycled plastic bottles, can be found everywhere and in a variety of colors. Or you can choose felt in natural fibers such as wool and bamboo (my fave!). Felt can be found in the craft section sold by the sheet (letter size), or in the yardage department sold on 72″-wide bolts.

Keep in mind synthetic felt melts, so always cover it with a cloth if you need to iron it.

Oilcloth

Oilcloth is regular cotton fabric fused with a thin layer of vinyl. It's perfect for making water-resistant, easy-wash items. The selection in fabric stores is generally limited, but you can find more online. There's also the option of making your own by ironing fusible vinyl to fabric, or asking a parent for a tablecloth made from oilcloth that you can cut! You can also use a solid-color vinyl totally made from plastic.

sewing supplies and tools

Basic Sewing Kit

1. Pins and pincushion

2. Fabric scissors

3. Thread snipers

4. Measuring tape

5. Flat ruler and/or regular ruler

6. Erasable fabric-marking pen
(My favorite: FriXion pens by Pilot!)

7. Chalk marker

8. Seam ripper

9. Tracing wheel

10. Point turner and presser

11. Hand sewing needles

12. Sewing machine needles

13. Safety pins

14. Awl

Hot Tools!

IRON AND HOT GLUE GUN Be super careful when you are using a tool that gets hot. Make sure you tell an adult that you are using it, and ask for help if you need it.

Optional Tools

EMBROIDERY NEEDLE A little thicker than regular hand sewing needle; you need it to sew with embroidery floss or perle cotton on the Dolman T-Shirt (page 63) and the Couching Stitch Pillow (page 58).

BALLPOINT SEWING MACHINE NEEDLE If you are sewing with stretch knit fabrics, you will need to change to this needle to sew jersey.

PARCHMENT PAPER OR TRACING PAPER These are for retracing patterns and placement diagrams. Lighter than regular printer paper, you can easily see through it. This makes tracing simple but also helps to position words and designs on your project, for example.

FABRIC GLUE STICK The glue will temporarily hold the string for the Couching Stitch Pillow.

BASTING GLUE SPRAY This spray will temporarily stick the doily to the apron for customization.

DOUBLE-SIDED FUSIBLE TAPE You use this tape with trims, zippers, or on very slippery fabrics that are hard to pin together.

KAMSNAPS AND PLIERS A colorful alternative to sewing on buttons for eyes; quick and easy to attach (see KAMsnaps, page 21). You can always find a substitute if you don't have this equipment.

NONSTICK PRESSER FOOT You can easily craft your own nonstick foot by using a piece of masking tape or washi tape on the bottom of a regular presser foot. Tear away the part of the tape that covers the opening in the presser foot; this is where the needle will need to pass through.

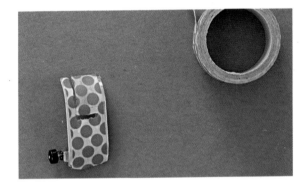

You can buy a presser foot for your machine that won't stick to vinyl, thanks to the Teflon surface under the foot. If you want to buy one, make sure it works with your model of machine.

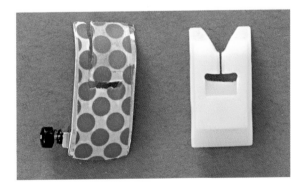

Optional Supplies

FUSIBLE INTERFACING Interfacing adds structure to fabric. Lightweight fusible interfacing gives a little body without causing the fabric to be stiff. It holds up well under normal wear and tear, and it washes and dries very well too.

Fusible interfacings are easy to use. Just remember that the textured side is always the sticky side. Apply the textured side to the wrong side of the fabric and press the whole area for a few seconds with an iron (see Hot Tools!, page 9). *Note: To properly fuse interfacing, press section by section, picking up and moving the iron rather than sliding it back and forth.* Flip the interfaced fabric over and press the fabric side.

CLEAR VINYL Clear vinyl is sold by the yard in 54˝-wide rolls. Pick light- or medium-weight vinyl rather than the heavier ones. It will be cheaper, much more flexible, and easier to sew with! If you have wrinkles or it tends to roll, place it under a flat, heavy surface, such as a pile of books. You can also use a hair dryer to heat and smooth the plastic, but never use an iron!

using arts and craft supplies on fabric

The use of markers, paint, and vinyl is a great way to add an element of fantasy to your project, and they lend an artistic, professional touch.

Fabric Markers

You can use fabric markers the same way you would use regular markers, but you need to know the ink is permanent and cannot be removed. To limit mistakes, first mark the design with an erasable fabric-marking pen (such as FriXion). Fabric markers dry very fast. Don't forget to set the ink by pressing with an iron (see Hot Tools!, page 9) for a few seconds. Over time, fabric marker designs can fade but you can easily go over them again and make them like new!

Fabric Paint

Fabric paint is like regular paint; it comes in hundreds of colors and you can mix them to create your own tones. But be careful! It's permanent and cannot be removed. Protect your clothes by rolling up your sleeves, putting on an apron, and covering your workspace.

1 ⋮ Prewash and dry the fabric. Press with an iron (see Hot Tools!, page 9).

2 ⋮ Lightly draw the design with a fabric-marking pen, if necessary.

3 ⋮ If you have 2 layers of fabric, insert cardboard or craft paper to protect the underneath layer from absorbing paint from the top layer.

4 ⋮ Paint the project with a regular paintbrush. To stencil, as I did on the Hand-Printed Apron (page 83), use a light tapping motion with a sponge paintbrush.

5 ⋮ Let it dry overnight.

6 ⋮ To remove any fabric pen marks and set the paint, press from the back and protect the painted side with a cloth.

7 ⋮ Let it dry for at least a week before you wash it the first time, and it will last wash after wash.

Puffy Paint

This multisurface dimensional paint comes in a variety of colors. You can use it on all types of fabric. It's very easy to use and it's really "mess-free." To produce a three-dimensional effect, use the narrow tip of the paint tube to paint the project. With its thin tip, you'll be able to trace very thin dimensional lines as a substitute for stitched embroidery lines or make puffy paint drops to create cute little eyes.

1 With the cap on, flip the bottle over and shake it up and down to bring all the paint to the tip (bubbles in the paint can be catastrophic). **A**

2 Open the bottle and apply it with the bottle slightly tilted and the tip against the surface. Barely press the tube to control the flow of paint. Use consistent pressure to apply the paint. **B**

3 Let it dry overnight and sometimes longer if you used a lot of paint.

TIP ● *If you mess up and drop paint by mistake, don't do anything—just let it dry. It will be easier to scratch off the dry paint than to try removing the wet paint.*

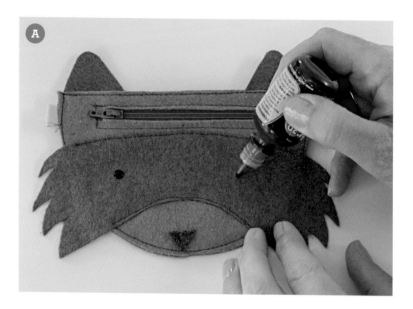

Fabric Chalkboard Paint

This type of paint must be used on small surfaces and on heavy-duty fabric because it tends to stiffen the fabric. (Cotton canvas is perfect.) Painting with chalkboard paint is a highly messy job. Protect your work area and don't forget to wear an apron.

1 : Frame the area you want to become a chalkboard with masking tape. **C**

2 : Apply chalkboard paint in generous quantities with a large sponge paintbrush. Paint in different directions—horizontally, vertically and diagonally—until the texture of the fabric is covered up. **D**

3 : Let it dry overnight. Apply an additional coat if necessary.

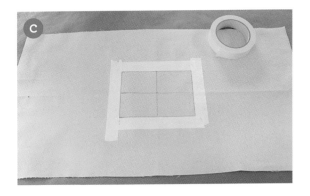

Glow-in-the-Dark Fabric Paint

Isn't it fantastic to have this option? This paint must be used on light-colored, heavy-duty fabric. (Cotton canvas is perfect.) Like chalkboard paint, glow-in-the-dark paint must be applied in generous quantities if you want a good glow. But this paint is not as messy as dark paint; it's transparent and barely even visible.

1 : With an erasable fabric-marking pen, trace the shape to paint. With a sponge brush, apply a generous coat of paint.

Let it dry overnight, then press the surface with an iron (see Hot Tools!, page 9) to erase the fabric-marking pen. Use a cloth between the fabric and the iron to protect the paint.

2 : Set the painted area in the light for a few minutes and it will glow in the dark for a while!

Iron-On Vinyl

Iron-on transfer sheets come in vibrant colors, shimmery finishes, and trendy patterns, perfect for achieving quick and easy, personalized designs for your apparel and home decor projects. Simply cut using scissors (or a cutting machine) and heat set the designs to your fabrics.

1 Trace the shape on the back of the vinyl. You can use a whiteboard marker, a high-lighter, or a simple marker if your fabric-marking pen is barely visible or doesn't work on vinyl. If you are using iron-on vinyl that comes with a clear plastic sheet covering the right side, you can trace the design on the front with a permanent marker; there's no need to trace on the back. **A**

2 With paper scissors or craft scissors, cut out the shape following the inner line of the drawing. Wipe off any remaining marks with a paper towel.

3 On the ironing board, place the sticky side of the vinyl on the right side of the project, taking care to position it correctly. Using a cloth to protect the vinyl, press the shape for a few seconds with an iron (see Hot Tools!, page 9). **B**

4 Flip the project over and press the vinyl from the back for a few seconds. You don't need the protective cloth for this part.

5 If your vinyl embellishment is for clothing, make it last longer by using coordinating thread to sew close to the edge all the way around the shape with a straight stitch. Stitch over the top of the beginning stitches about 1″ to anchor the stitching. If you are making a home decor item that will not be washed frequently, you can skip this step. **C**

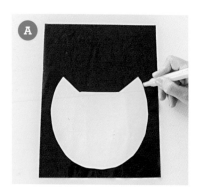

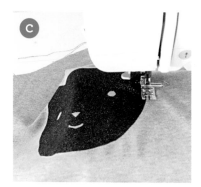

Sewing Techniques

hemming cotton fabric

1 Keep the project turned inside out. Fold the hem's raw edge up approximately ½˝ and press with an iron (see Hot Tools!, page 9). Fold it up another 1˝ and press again. Pin all the way around.

2 If your machine has an extended table or accessory box that can be removed, set it aside to expose the free arm of the machine. Set the machine up for a straight stitch. Begin stitching close to the garment's side seam where the stop and start is less likely to show. With the left edge of the presser foot aligned to the hem's folded edge, sew as straight as you can all the way around the hem with a large straight stitch (3 to 3.5). Sew over the top of the beginning stitches about 1˝ to secure them.

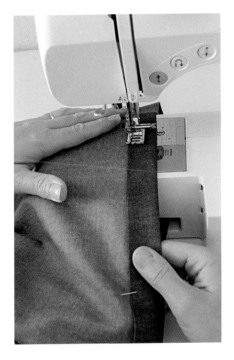

hemming knit fabric

1 With the garment inside out, fold the raw edge of the opening over and press with an iron (see Hot Tools!, page 9). Use a ½˝ fold for sleeves, necklines, and other small sections. For bottom hems, fold up 1˝.

2 If your machine has an extended table or accessory box that can be removed, set it aside. Set the machine up for a narrow zigzag stitch (length 2 and width 3.5). Place the presser foot so the edge of the zigzag stitch will be right on the raw edge of the fabric. Sew all the way around the opening. Turn the garment right side out and give it a nice press.

running stitch

This is the most basic hand stitch ever! You just have to pass the threaded needle in and out of the fabric along the stitching line. For a nice-looking running stitch, make even stitches all the way along. I used the running stitch in the Donut Pillow (page 42), the Glow-in-the-Dark Light Bulb (page 54), and the Dolman T-Shirt (page 63).

1 Thread a needle and tie a knot at the other end. Push the needle up from underneath the fabric. Ⓐ

2 With the needle on top of the fabric, decide the size of the stitches and the space between them. If you decide to make ¼″ stitches, push the needle down ¼″ away from where you brought it up. Bring the needle up from the back with the same ¼″ spacing. Ⓑ

3 Keep sewing this way until the end of the stitching line. Finish with the needle on the back so you can tie a knot in the thread, preferably as close as possible to the fabric. Ⓒ

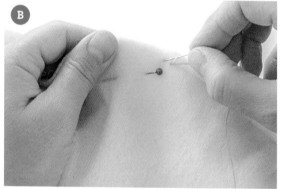

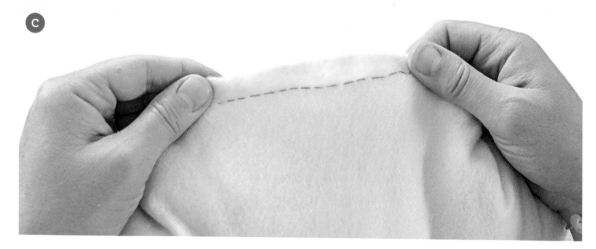

whipstitch

The whipstitch can be nearly invisible the closer you insert the needle to the edge of the fabric. I use the whipstitch to close the no-sew zone (page 18) after a project has been turned right side out.

NOTE: Thread Color *Here I used a contrasting thread color so you can see the stitches, but I encourage you to use a thread matching the main color of the fabric.*

1 : Thread the needle and tie a knot at the end of the thread. Turn all the raw edges of a no-sew zone under and stack the fabric folds, one on top of the other. Push the needle up from the back of the fabric and pull it through one fold until the knot stops against the back of the fabric invisible to the front side.

2 : Then push the needle through the edge of both folded layers and repeat with even

stitches until you have completely joined the 2 pieces of fabric. **D**

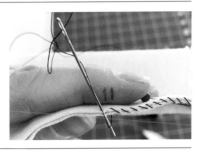

TIP ● *You can draw two little lines on your index finger as a guide to help you stitch consistently.*

3 : Here's how to tie a knot at the end: When you finish the last stitch, don't pull the thread entirely through the fabric. Instead, keep a small loop of thread, put the needle through it, and pull the thread tight to tie a knot. Repeat with a second loop and knot. **E**

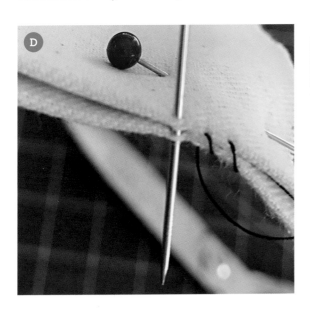

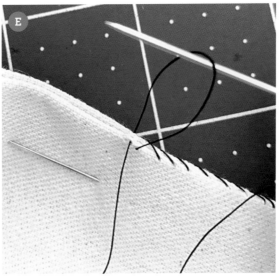

no-sew zone

This is an unsewn gap in stitching that is used to turn the project inside out. Each pattern comes with a suggested location that will be a hidden area of the finished project.

1 Mark the no-sew zone with an erasable fabric-marking pen.

2 Start sewing at one end of the no-sew zone, and sew all around the project until you reach the other side of the no-sew zone, backstitching at the beginning and end. Or if the no-sew zone is on just one side of the project, sew the first part of the seam until the no-sew zone mark; then backstitch. Restart sewing on the opposite side of the no-sew zone, backstitching at the beginning and end of the seam. **A**

3 Once the project is turned right side out, close the seam with a hand-sewn whipstitch (page 17) or sew a straight stitch very close to the folded edges by machine. **B**

TIP ● Reinforcing the No-Sew Zone

With delicate fabrics (such as flannel or thin cotton) or very stiff material (such as vinyl or oilcloth), use this simple stitching technique to make it easier to pull the fabric through the hole: When you reach the no-sew zone, pivot at a right angle and sew toward the edge of the fabric. Backstitch to secure the stitching. Repeat on the other side, sewing away from the edge of the fabric and then turning to sew the seam. This reinforces the seam and the fabric.

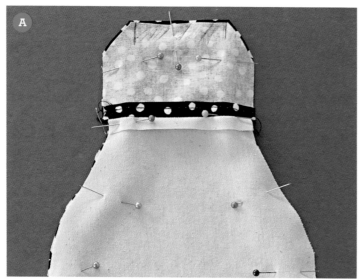

No-sew zone marked

fusible appliqué

1 On the paper backing of the fusible web, draw your design in a size that fits your shirt.

2 At the ironing board, place the sticky side of the fusible to the wrong side of the fabric (paper side facing you) and press with an iron (see Hot Tools!, page 9) a few seconds to fuse in place. **C**

TIP ● *Your design will be reversed when the fusible web is placed on the wrong side of the fabric. This means that if you draw letters or another design that is asymmetrical (meaning it* cannot *be reversed and still be correct, such as the letter B, as opposed to the letter O), be sure to reverse the design before you trace it.*

---

3 Once the fabric has cooled down, cut out the shape you drew on the paper. Peel off the backing paper. **D**

4 Place the wrong, fusible side of the appliqué onto the right side of the background fabric. Press the shape a few seconds again, making sure the placement is correct prior to fusing it in place.

5 Set up the sewing machine to do a very narrow zigzag stitch (length 0.9 and width 4–5) with a coordinating thread color. Place the presser foot very close to the edge and sew all the way around, taking care to stay on the edge of the shape. Continue sewing over the beginning stitches about 1˝. **E**

TIP ● *If this is your first time sewing an appliqué in place, practice on scraps to check your machine settings and gain confidence.*

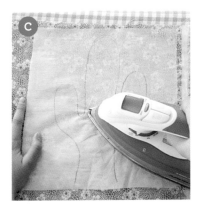

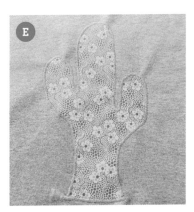

making a tassel

A tassel is a bundle of loose threads or cords knotted at one end that attaches to curtains, clothing, necklaces, or other items as decoration. Tassels are easy to make, using a similar technique in creating pom-poms (see Note: Pom-Poms, at right). You can use cording, yarn, embroidery floss, or T-shirt yarn. They add a nice touch of whimsy.

Regular Tassel

1⋮ Wrap multiple strands of yarn around your hand until the yarn bundle is as big you want the tassel. Remove the loop from your hand. **Ⓐ**

2⋮ Use a 20˝-long strand, double it, pass it through the loop, and tie it with a double knot to secure the top of the bundle. **Ⓑ**

3⋮ Wrap a 10˝ strand around the top of the tassel and tie a knot as tight as you can. (An additional hand would be helpful for this step!) **Ⓒ**

4⋮ Give shape to the tassel by cutting the loops, any excess at the top, and trimming the ends. **Ⓓ**

NOTE
Pom-Poms *Making a pom-pom is similar to making a tassel. The only difference is that you wrap more yarn around your hand for more bulk, you tie all the loops together in the middle with a double knot, and you cut the loops on both side of the knot. Trim and fluff to create the pom-pom. Voilà!*

Loops secured around the middle

Fluffed and shaped

Felt Tassel

1 Cut fringes into the long side of a felt rectangle.

2 Tightly roll the rectangle along the uncut side to the size you want the tassel. **E**

3 With coordinating thread, sew the top section together by pushing the needle through all layers several times. Finally, bring the thread up through the center.

4 Create a thread loop for attaching the tassel to your project, and tie a knot. **F**

KAMsnaps

If you want to quickly attach snaps, KAMsnaps are a frustration-free alternative compared to buttons or classic metal snaps. They are plastic, very easy to install, and come in various colors and shapes. You can also customize them with a permanent marker (great for making eyes). To attach them, you'll need KAMsnaps basic pliers, which you can find in fabric stores or online. It's an investment, but you won't regret it when you see the benefits. The pliers set may come with an awl and some plastic snaps.

For each snap, you'll need 2 caps, 1 socket, and 1 stud. Make sure your pliers match the size of the snaps. I used size 20 snaps.

1 Refer to the pattern to see where to place the snap. Use an awl to create a small hole in the fabric.

2 Insert a cap's spindle through the hole and place a socket onto the spindle on the other side of the hole.

3 Keep the cap side down and place it in the pliers' receptacle. Squeeze the pliers. Repeat the process to place a cap and stud on the opposite side of the closure. Once you have installed each side of the snap, test it. If either side feels loose, simply insert it in the pliers again and squeeze.

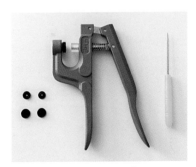

KAMsnap components, basic pliers, awl

using an embroidery hoop

1 An embroidery hoop is composed of 2 circles—the inner and the outer hoop—held together with a screw on the outer hoop. Unscrew the screw a little and separate the 2 hoops.

2 Center the sewing area of your project over the inner hoop with the fabric right side up. **Ⓐ**

3 Loosen the screw of the outer hoop and place the hoop around the inner hoop capturing the fabric in between. Push it down to firmly tuck the fabric in the hoop. If you have trouble making it go over the inner hoop, loosen the screw some more.

4 Tighten the screw so that the fabric is held firmly in place between the hoops. Take care not to overstretch knit fabrics. **Ⓑ**

measuring for garments

You'll need to take your measurements for the clothing section. Use a measuring tape over undergarments but not over other clothes. Complete the table with your measurements and find the size that best matches your measurements.

CHEST Measure around the fullest part of your chest (lift your arms slightly).

WAIST Measure around your waistline at the level you normally wear your pants.

HIPS Measure around the fullest part of your hips.

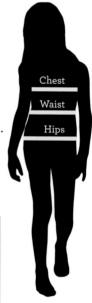

Chest
Waist
Hips

Body Size Chart

Youth size	8	10	12	14	16	My size
Bust/chest	29˝ (74 cm)	30˝ (76.2 cm)	31˝ (79 cm)	32˝ (81.3 cm)	33˝ (84 cm)	
Waist	23½˝ (60.5 cm)	24˝ (61 cm)	24½˝ (62.5 cm)	25˝ (63.7 cm)	25½˝ (65 cm)	
Hips	30˝ (76.2 cm)	31˝ (79 cm)	32˝ (81.3 cm)	33˝ (84 cm)	34˝ (86.5 cm)	

working with patterns

Before you trace or cut a pattern, pay attention to all specific markings and terms. It's very important to transfer the marks onto the fabric; they will be invaluable help when cutting and sewing.

FOLD   If you see "Fold" along an outer line of the pattern, it means you have to fold the fabric and lay that edge of the pattern on the fold before you cut out the pattern piece. *Do not cut along the line marked fold!* The goal is to create a full front or back without having to sew a seam.

CUTTING LINE   This is the outer line of the pattern, unless it is marked "Fold" (see paragraph above). In multisize patterns, choose the line that corresponds to your size. The seam allowance is included, so just cut on the line.

GRAINLINE ARROW   This is a line with arrow points at both ends. Always place the pattern piece with this double arrow running parallel to the selvage, the tightly woven edge of the fabric where the manufacturer prints information. Use a ruler or measuring tape to measure the distance from the selvage to the line at both ends of the arrow to be sure you have placed the pattern correctly.

NOTCH   This little V- or double V-shaped mark can be found on the edge of the cutting line and tells you where to match the different pieces to sew together.

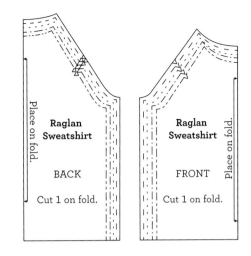

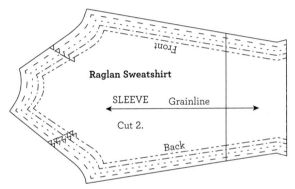

————————	16 year-old
– – – – –	14 year-old
· · · · · · · · ·	12 year-old
–·—·—·—·	10 year-old
——··——··——	8 year-old

useful terms

Right Sides Together

When you look at fabric, there are two sides to it. The *right side* is the front where the color is vibrant and the pattern is strongest. The *wrong side* is the back of the fabric where the pattern and colors are weaker and muted. So when you are instructed to sew right sides together, it means you put the right sides of two fabrics together—one on top of the other. This means that one of the wrong sides will be facing you.

Seam Allowance

The seam allowance is between the raw edge of the fabric and the stitched line. To make it simple, most seam allowances in this book are measured by the width of a regular presser foot, about ⅜″–½″. To sew, just keep the edge of the presser foot lined up with the edge of the fabric. The pattern directions will tell you when to use a different measurement.

If you need to use a different seam allowance, you can sometimes move the needle left or right to adjust its distance from the edge of the fabric. If you don't have this option, place a piece of washi tape on the machine bed at the desired distance from the needle and line the fabric up with it as you sew.

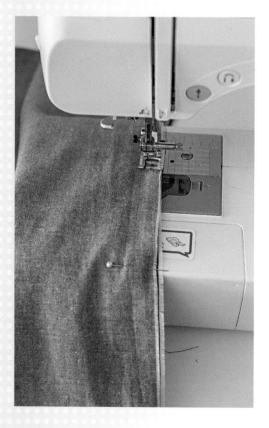

guide to skill levels

Beginner-friendly

A good project for those who are just starting to use the sewing machine or who want something easy to make.

Some experience required

A project for someone who is used to sewing on a machine. These will be more sophisticated, requiring patience, more time, and perhaps some hand sewing.

May I have some help, please?

You may need to ask for some help as you learn the new techniques in these projects. You can do it; you just have to be open to taking the extra time to learn new skills.

downloading patterns

Some project patterns can be found in the pullouts that come with this book, but many others are available as online PDFs to download and print using your personal printer. These can be found at the following web address:

tinyurl.com/11313-patterns-download

animal neck pillow

Beginner-friendly

9″ wide × 2½″ high × 8″ deep

Raccoon, fox, or bunny for the next trip, anyone? Useful and pretty, you won't want to miss bringing the sweetest neck pillow along for a relaxing journey!

- Solid-color flannel, 1 rectangle 18″ × 21″

- Interfacing, 1 rectangle 18″ × 21″

- Coordinating felt, at least 8″ × 11″ rectangle

- Polyfill stuffing

- Fabric markers for customizing face and body

- Basic sewing kit (page 8)

⚠ Hot Tools (page 9)

- Hot glue gun for attaching bunny tail

- Iron

Patterns

- Download and print the Animal Neck Pillow patterns (body, tail, and ear) and placement diagram (face) for the bunny, fox, or raccoon. (See Downloading Patterns, page 25.)

Note: If you are making the pillow for a teen-ager or adult, print out the pattern enlarged to 120% instead.

prepare the pieces

1 ⋮ Press the interfacing and flannel together with an iron. Place the sticky side of the inter-facing on the wrong side of the flannel. With a dry, hot iron (turn the steam setting off), press a few seconds to fuse in place. (For more information, see Fusible Interfacing, page 10.)

TIP ● *Most of the time, it's hard to tell the right from the wrong side of flannel. But if you can feel a difference in texture, consider the softer side as the right side.*

2 ⋮ Fold the flannel piece with fused inter-facing in half along the grainline. Place the pattern on the fold and trace it. Cut out the neck pillow, but do not cut along the fold line. Repeat a second time. Ⓐ You now have a back and a front for the neck pillow.

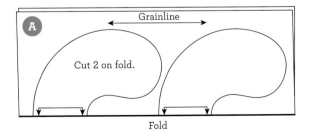

3 : Trace all the small body parts of your chosen animal onto felt. **B**

You will need:

• 1 pair of ears • 4 legs • 1 tail

Note: For the bunny tail, you can craft a pom-pom (page 20) with yarn, and then hot glue it to the neck pillow.

Cut the pieces out nice and smooth.

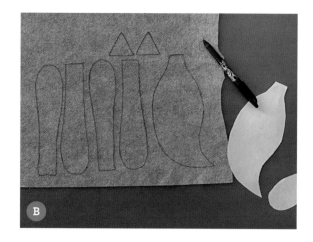

step by step

It's easy to make ⅜″–½″ seam allowances: Just line up the edge of a regular sewing foot with the edge of the fabric.

1 : If you are making the raccoon or fox, pin the ears and tail onto the right side of the pillow front. If you are making the bunny, wait and place the tail later. **C**

2 : Pin the front and back legs onto the right side of the pillow back.

3 : Sew the body parts placed on the front (ears and tail) and back (legs) of the pillow with coordinating thread. Topstitch about a ¼″ from the edge to secure. Backstitch at the beginning and end of each short stitching line.

4 : Place both pieces in front of you right side up, and fold the back legs and tail toward the inside so they will be out of the way of the seam allowance. Pin. **D**

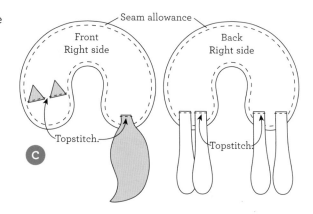

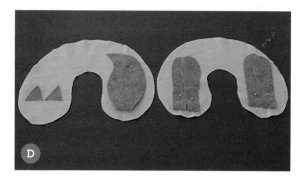

5 : Match the front and back pillow pieces right sides together. The edges should be perfectly even. Check to be sure the tail and legs are out of the seamline. Pin. **E**

6 : Mark the no-sew zone (page 18) on the inside curve of the pillow. This gap is essential for turning and stuffing the pillow.

(page 18)

> **NOTE**
> **Pinning** *Pinning can be done several ways. When using fabrics with slippery pile, it's best to pin in the seamline, all pins facing the same direction. The sewing machine needle will approach the pin from the sharp point. Pull the pin out before the sewing machine needle gets to it. If you pin the opposite way, you'll have a hard time removing the pins as the needle comes!*

7 : Starting at one end of the no-sew zone, stitch carefully all around the pillow to the opposite side. Backstitch at the beginning and end. **F**

8 : Check your work on the finished side. If it looks good, return to the wrong side and snip the curves in the seam allowance, taking care not to clip into the stitching. Snipping helps to ease the fabric so the seam lies flat. **G**

9 : Turn the pillow right side out and stuff with polyfill, making it firm around the neck.

10 : Use a whipstitch (page 17) and coordinating thread to close the no-sew zone. **H**

(page 17)

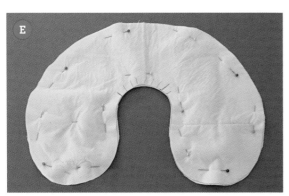

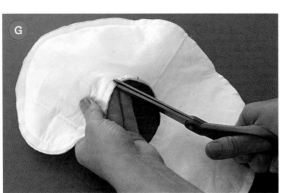

11 Now, you can design the face of the animal neck pillow. Look at the patterns for the face designs, and draw some marks on the body as you see in the photo. 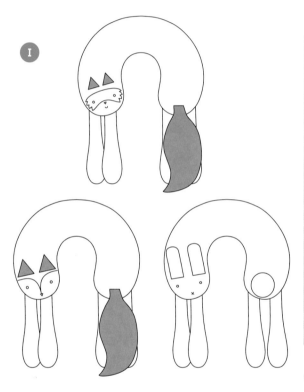 **I**

Lightly draw the face on, like a rough sketch, with an erasable fabric pen. Use a chalk marker rather than a FriXion pen on dark flannel, because FriXion tends to bleach and leave marks.

12 Trace the sketch with permanent fabric markers. Press the design with an iron to heat-set the ink and make it last longer. **J** If you made the bunny, now make a pom-pom tail (page 20) and use the hot glue gun to attach it.

● ● ● ● ● ● ● ● ● ● ● ● ● ● ● ● ▶ *Bon voyage!*

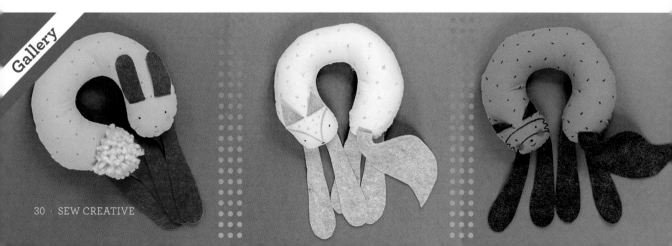

critter coin pouch 6″ × 4″

Some experience required

Which woodland critter would you trust to take care of your money? This zipper pouch is easy to sew, fun to create, and simple to make, with a cord shoulder strap if you want to use it as a purse. There are patterns for a raccoon, bunny, or fox face, but feel free to draw up a different animal!

- Felt, 1 piece at least 15″ × 6″ and some small scraps for ears and mask

- Black KAMsnaps (page 21) or puffy paint (page 12) for eyes

- Zipper, at least 5″ long

- Zipper foot

- Basic sewing kit (page 8)

⚠ Hot Tools (page 9)

- Hot glue gun

- Iron

Optional items

- Double-sided fusible tape

- Double-fold bias tape, 3″ length to attach shoulder strap

- 5 mm (about ¼″) cording, about 5-foot length for shoulder strap

- Small pom-pom for animal nose

Patterns

- Download and print the Critter Coin Pouch patterns (front, back, face mask, and ear) and placement diagram (face) for the bunny, fox, or raccoon. (See Downloading Patterns, page 25.)

prepare the pieces

1 : Pick an animal (or make your own). Cut out the following pattern pieces from felt.

• 1 pouch front and back

• 2 ears

• 1 animal face mask of the bunny, fox, or raccoon

2 : Trace the rectangle for the zipper onto the pouch front only.

step by step

It's easy to make ⅜″–½″ seam allowances: Just line up the edge of a regular sewing foot with the edge of the fabric.

For these project instructions, I chose the raccoon.

1 : Cut out the 4″ × ½″ rectangle for the zipper opening that you traced onto the front pouch. To do this, fold the piece of felt in half and make a small cut into the interior of the rectangle, large enough to insert a pair of scissors. Now you can properly cut along the traced line. You can also carefully rip the felt with a seam ripper to make room for the scissors. Ⓐ

2 Cut 2 pieces of double-sided fusible tape, each 4″ long. Lay them along the right side of the zipper. Using medium heat, press each a few seconds with an iron and then peel off the paper backing.

3 On the ironing board, place the open rectangle on top of the zipper. If you have placed it correctly, you should see only the teeth of the zipper through the opening. Press with the iron to fuse them together.

4 Attach a zipper foot to the sewing machine. With the front piece facing up, sew all the way around the zipper opening. Keep the edge of the presser foot close to the edge of the rectangle.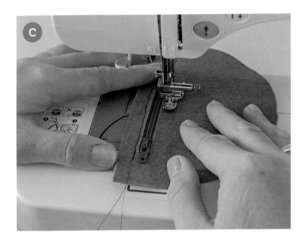

5 Pin the raccoon's felt face mask on the pouch front, as shown on the placement diagram. Using coordinating thread, sew the top and bottom of the mask to the pouch, nice and close to the mask's edge. For the raccoon, start and stop the stitching about ½″ before reaching the outer edges of the pouch front. This is because you will need to lift the face mask and stitch underneath it to finish the pouch.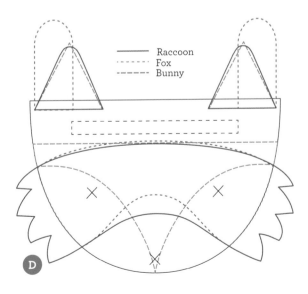

6 If you want snaps for eyes, it's time to attach the KAMsnaps (page 21). If you would like to paint the eyes on, wait until you finish sewing the pouch. Follow the placement diagram for positioning.

—— Raccoon
----- Fox
-- -- Bunny

7 Line up the pouch back and front together, and then insert the ears as shown on the placement diagram (page 33). Pin in place. **E**

You can make this pouch with or without a shoulder strap. If you want a strap, go to Step 8. If you do *not* want a strap, skip to Step 9.

8 With a shoulder strap:

To make the pouch with a shoulder strap, sew the top of the pouch together first to secure the ears in place. Cut 2 pieces of 1½˝ bias tape, and fold each piece in half. Insert a bias tape loop between the layers on each side and pin them in place. Sew around the rest of the pouch, nice and close to the edge. Be sure to sew over the bias loops to attach them to the pouch. Now skip to Step 10. **F**

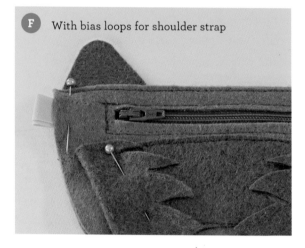

F With bias loops for shoulder strap

9 Without a shoulder strap:

Sew all the way around the pouch, nice and close to the edge. For the raccoon, pin the mask out of the way of the seam first.

10 You are almost done! If you didn't use KAMsnaps as eyes (see Step 6), use puffy paint now. (A great alternative!) Make 2 small drops of black puffy paint on the marks shown on the pattern. Let it dry overnight. Hot glue a small pom-pom or a tiny piece of felt in place for the nose. **G**

Congrats! Your critter coin pouch is alive! ● ● ● ● ● ● ● ● ● ● ● ● ● ● ● ●▶

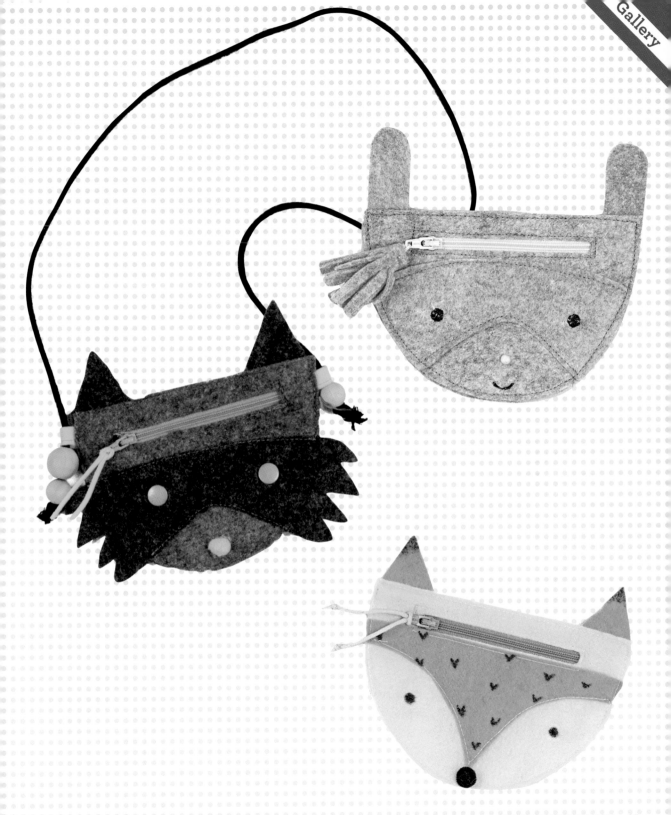

chalkboard backpack

15½˝ × 13˝

Some experience required

Making a backpack may sound complicated to you. But don't worry, this one is quick and easy.

- Medium- or heavyweight cotton fabric, 1 yard, cut into 2 rectangles 14˝ × 32˝

  Another option: Use 2 different fabrics: 1 for outer bag and 1 for lining, ½ yard each (*Note: If your fabric is directional, you may have to cut the rectangles along the length of grain.*)

- Heavyweight unbleached cotton cloth (canvas), 1 square 8˝ × 8˝

- Black chalkboard paint for fabric

- Masking tape

- Sponge brush

- 5 mm (about ¼˝) cording, 4-yard length

- Decorative trim (even trim with small hanging pom-poms or fringe, for example), 9˝ length

- Basic sewing kit (page 8)

⚠ Hot Tools (page 9)

- Iron

prepare the pieces

1 Use a tight zigzag stitch to finish the edges of the 8˝ canvas square.

2 Protect your work area with newspaper or drop cloth, and wear an apron. Paint one side of the canvas with a generous coat of black chalkboard paint. Let it dry overnight.

step by step

It's easy to make ⅜″–½″ seam allowances: Just line up the edge of a regular sewing foot with the edge of the fabric.

1 ⋮ Center a 9″ strip of decorative trim along one edge of the chalkboard square. Let the trim hang slightly over each side while you sew it to the square, but tuck the cut ends under the back when you are done. Pin in place or use double-sided fusible tape as I did for the Critter Coin Pouch zipper (page 31).

2 ⋮ If your trim is especially bumpy, select the zipper foot for the sewing machine. Using a straight stitch, sew the top of the trim close to the edge of the chalkboard square. Otherwise you can zigzag most trims to the top of the square. If you need to, change back to the regular presser foot. Ⓐ

3 ⋮ Fold the outer bag rectangle in half so it measures 14″ × 16″. Place it in front of you with the folded edge closest to you. The right side of the front panel should be facing you, so if the fabric is directional, be sure the motif is right side up. Center the chalkboard square from side to side; its bottom edge should be 2″ above the backpack's fold. The decorative trim should be at the top. Mark its position, then unfold the backpack fabric and pin the chalkboard square to the single layer of the backpack's front where you marked it. Ⓑ

4 ⋮ Sew around the sides and bottom to create a pocket. Backstitch at the beginning and end.

5 Refold the outer bag in half, but this time right sides together. Pin and sew the sides together.

6 Repeat Step 5 with the lining rectangle but mark a 4˝ no-sew zone (page 18) near the bottom of one side. Turn the stitched lining inside out, so the right side is facing you. **C**

7 Insert the lining into the outer bag. Match up both bags at the bottom crease. Align the side seams of the outer bag and lining and pin the top edges together. **D**

8 If you have an open-arm sewing machine, remove the extended table or accessory box and set it aside. Slide the top of the bag onto the machine. Sew all the way around the top edge of the bag.

9 Turn the bag inside out through the no-sew zone. Fold the edges of the no-sew zone in, even with the seams on either side of the opening. Press the fabric with an iron to keep the folds you made. On the machine, sew the gap closed by sewing a straight stitch very close to the edge.

10 Push the lining down into the outer bag and push the corners out. Press the seam at the top of the bag, but be careful to avoid the chalkboard pocket; you don't want to mess up the paint or the iron! **E**

11 Lightly draw a line 1˝ from the top of the bag. Use an erasable marking pen. Sew all the way around to create a casing. **F**

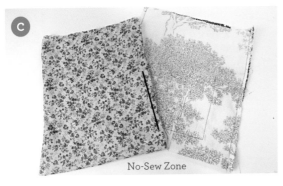

No-Sew Zone

12 : On the outside of the bag, use a seam ripper to carefully remove the stitching from both casing side seams of the backpack's outer layer (not the lining). **G**

13 : Cut the cord into 2-yard lengths. Attach a safety pin at the end of one length of cord and use it to guide the cord through one of casing's openings, around and back out the same opening. Repeat with the second cord and the second casing opening on the other side of the bag. **H**

14 : Align the cords and knot the ends together on each side. **I**

15 : Turn the backpack inside out. Make a mark 1˝ from the bottom corner on both the bottom and the side seams. Use an erasable fabric-marking tool and draw a line from mark to mark to create a triangle. Do the same for the second bottom corner. **J**

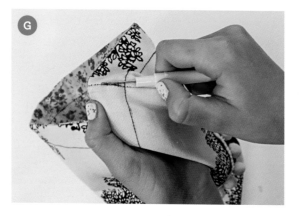

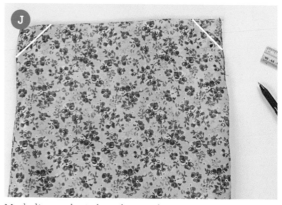

Mark diagonal stitching lines at bottom corners.

16 From the right side, push the knotted end of the cords into the bottom corner of the bag. You will need to put your hand inside the bag to catch the knots and pin them to the corners.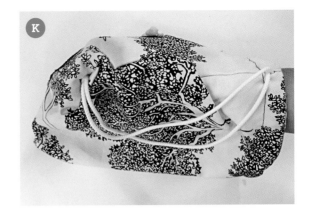

17 Sew on the lines you marked to enclose the knots. Go easy on the sewing machine. It will be an uneven surface as you stitch through the cording. Try to avoid the knots!

You are done!

Try out the bag and mark or draw whatever you want on the chalkboard!

Gallery

donut pillow 18˝ in diameter × 4½˝ deep

Beginner-friendly

Make the biggest, coziest and yummiest donut! Have fun spreading sprinkles, colors, and glitter on the icing! Or if you love kawaii-style (like Hello Kitty), choose a cute kitty, bunny, or piglet donut.

- Felt:

  Option 1: Iced donut: 2 yards cream for donut front and back; plus 1 yard pink for icing

  Option 2: Animal donut: 2 yards solid color for donut front and back (or 1 yard cream for donut back and 1 yard another solid color for donut front); plus scraps for ears, nose, eyes, tail, spots, or anything else you can think of to make your animal

- Chalk marker

- Polyfill stuffing

- Fabric paint (page 11), puffy paint (page 12), or both

- Cotton swabs

- Basic sewing kit (page 8)

 Hot Tools (page 9)

- Iron

Patterns

- Download and print the Donut Pillow patterns (donut; icing, if needed). For the Animal Donut Pillow, also download and print the ears pattern and placement diagram for the bunny, kitty, or pig. (See Downloading Patterns, page 25.) Tape the pages together where necessary.

prepare the pieces

1 Cut 2 felt circles 21˝ in diameter in your chosen colors for the donut front and back.

2 **Iced donut** Cut out 1 pink icing circle.

  Animal donut Cut out a pair of ears or any other small pieces you would like to add.

3 With a chalk marker or erasable fabric-marking pen, trace a 4˝ circle in the center of the front and back donut pieces, and in the icing as well, if you are making the iced donut.

TIP ● *To find the center of a circle, fold the circle in half and then in half again and mark the tip—that is the center!*

---

step by step

It's easy to make ⅜″–½″ seam allowances: Just line up the edge of a regular sewing foot with the edge of the fabric.

Iced Donut

1 : Center and pin the icing on top of 1 felt circle. **Ⓐ**

2 : With coordinating thread, sew all the way around the edge of the icing, nice and close to the edge.

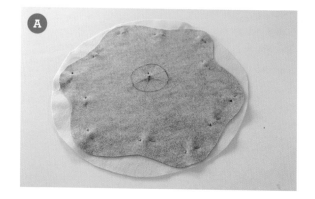

Animal Donut

1 : Pin the ears in place according to the placement markings on the pattern.

2 : Topstitch along the bottom edge of each ear with coordinating thread close to the edge. Backstitch at the beginning and end. Wait until the donut is sewn and stuffed to draw the face on. **Ⓑ**

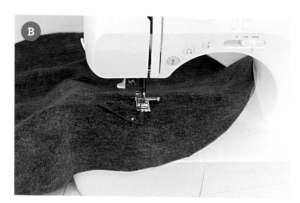

Donut Assembly

1 : Place the front and back circles wrong sides together, with the icing or the face of the animal on top. Pin the middle. Sew around the inner circle on the traced line. **Ⓒ**

2 : Press with an iron to remove the erasable fabric-marking pen marks around the inner circle. With a seam ripper, carefully cut into the middle of the inner circle. Insert scissors and create a center hole by cutting close to the seam.

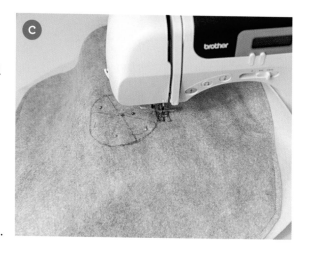

3 Pin all the way around the outer edges and mark a 3″ no-sew zone (page 18) to leave an opening for stuffing the donut. **D**

4 Stitch from one end of the no-sew zone all the way around the pillow to the other end of the no-sew zone, backstitching at the beginning and end.

5 Fill the donut with stuffing.

6 Pin the gap closed and hand sew it with a running stitch (page 16). **E**

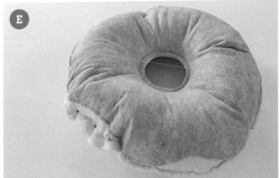

Customization

ICED DONUT Have fun decorating a yummy donut full of sprinkles. With fabric paint or puffy paint, make colorful polka dots and short lines, as if you were sprinkling confetti on the icing.

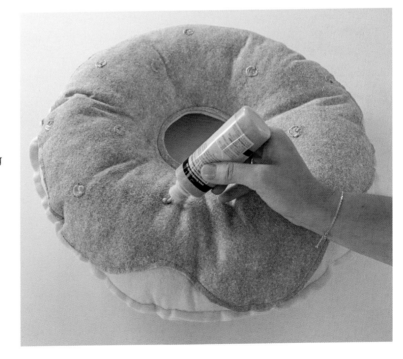

ANIMAL DONUT Center the placement diagram below the ears. You can push straight pins through the diagram to mark the eyes, nose, and whiskers. Then with an erasable fabric pen or a chalk marker, mark the pin positions on the felt. Use these marks for reference points and draw out the face freehand. Now you can use fabric markers or fabric paint to go over lines and make the face permanent.

Let them dry overnight. Enjoy!

TIP ● *I love to use cotton swabs to paint tiny little dots for the eyes and thin whiskers.*

Gallery

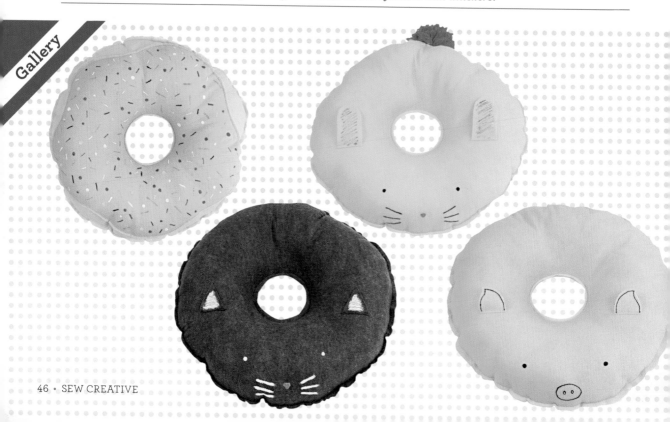

mermaid tail blanket

23˝ wide at flipper (19˝ wide at top of tail) × 48˝ long

Some experience required

Splash in your chilling time! Comfy, cozy, and fun, this blanket can be used like a sleeping bag. And did you know this blanket could glow in the dark?

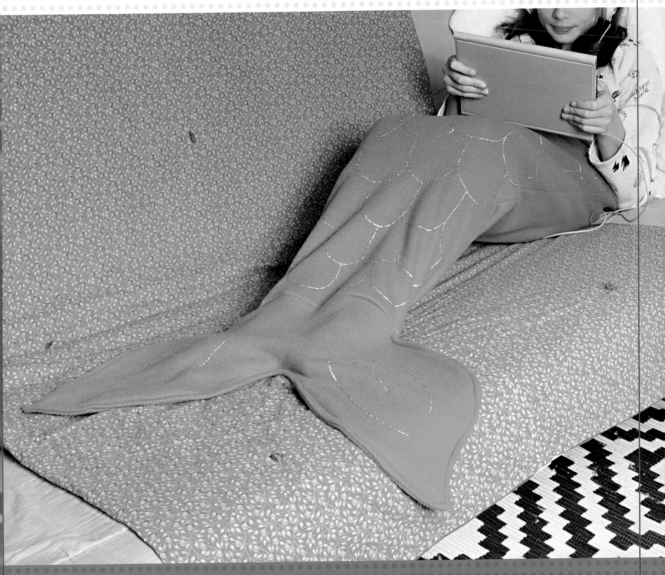

- Solid color fleece, 58″ wide, 1 yard

- Ballpoint sewing machine needle (14/90) or universal needle in large size (16/100)

- Basic sewing kit (page 8)

⚠ **Hot Tools (page 9)**

- Iron

Optional

- Fabric paint (page 11), puffy paint (page 12), or glow-in-the-dark fabric paint (page 13) for scales

Patterns

- Use the Mermaid Tail Blanket flipper pattern (pullout page P1).

TIP ● *Most of the time, fleece has no distinct right or wrong side. If you notice one side is fluffier than the other, use the smoothest side as the right side. The smoother the fabric, the easier it will be to paint the scale details!*

prepare the pieces

This Mermaid Tail Blanket has two sections: the tail and the flipper. *Note: To fit the tail and the flipper on the fabric (as shown in the cutting diagram, at right), keep the fabric folded in half lengthwise (the way it came when you bought it). Also make sure the stretch is crosswise.*

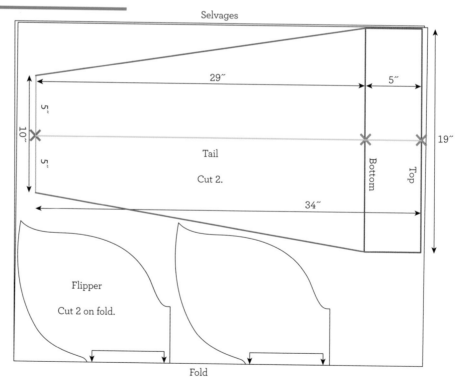

Flipper

With the flipper pattern, place the side marked "Fold" on the fold of the fabric (see the diagram on the previous page) and trace around it with an erasable fabric-marking pen. Trace another flipper. *Do not cut out the flippers yet.*

TIP ● *If it's hard to trace on fleece with the fabric-marking pen, you can use regular chalk. You can even sharpen the chalk with a pencil sharpener, if you have a sharpener for large pencils.*

Tail

Using the measurements in the diagram, you will measure and draw the tail onto the fabric with an erasable fabric-marking pen or chalk marker. A yardstick will come in handy.

1 Draw a 5″ × 19″ rectangle (see the **purple lines** in the diagram). The 5″ side of the rectangle should be parallel and as close to the selvage as possible.

2 Find the center of the rectangle's long side. It should be at 9½″. Mark this spot with an X on *both* long sides of the rectangle (see the **2 blue X's** in the diagram).

3 With the yardstick, line up the 2 X's and draw a line as straight as you can all the way down the yardstick (see the **yellow line** in

the diagram). Maybe you can find someone to hold the yardstick steady for you while you draw this line.

4 Measure from the X on the bottom of the rectangle 29″ along the line that you just drew. Mark this point with another X (see the **red X** in the diagram). This X is the middle of the 10″ line.

5 Line up the 5″ mark on the yardstick to the red X. Draw a 10″ line (the **green line** in the diagram) *perpendicular* to the long yellow line. The 2 lines together should look like a big letter T. This is where the mermaid's flipper will be attached.

6 The ends of the 10″ line give you the points you need to draw the final sides of the mermaid's tail. Using the yardstick, connect the bottom corners of the rectangle to each side of the 10″ line (see the **pink lines** in the diagram). Voilà, you have the mermaid's tail!

7 Make sure the flippers are not crossing over the tail lines. If they are, retrace the flippers to move them out of the way. Cut out along the *outside* lines of the tail. You can cut the 2 pieces simultaneously. Then cut out the 2 flippers.

step by step

It's easy to make ⅜″–½″ seam allowances: Just line up the edge of a regular sewing foot with the edge of the fabric.

1 Lay out a tail section right side up. Pin a flipper to the tail, right sides together, aligning the top of the flipper with the narrow end of the tail. Repeat for the second tail and flipper. **A**

2 Prep your sewing machine for sewing stretch fabrics. Insert a large needle for stretch fabric into the sewing machine and use your machine's extended table if you have one. Thread the machine with a color matching the fleece and set the stitch for a large zigzag (length 2 and width 5.5)—a zigzag seam won't break as you stretch out the blanket.

3 Sew the flippers and tails together, back-stitching at the beginning and end. **B**

Now, you have 2 identical panels, the front and back of blanket. Press the seam with an iron toward the top of the tail on each panel to make it flatter. This will help you sew across these bulky seams more easily.

4 Align the front and back of the blanket right sides together, with the tail section on your left and the flipper on your right. Make sure the front and back are perfectly even, matching the seams and the flippers. For easier stitching, sew the tail in 2 sections, half at a time. Pin half of the blanket closest to you, from the center of the flipper to the very top of the tail section. **C**

5 Because you are not sewing with the stretch of the fabric, a straight stitch will work best here. Set up a large straight stitch at 3.5 (7 stitches per inch), to handle the thickness of the fleece. Start sewing in the middle of the flipper, pivoting at the pointed tip of the flipper and heading up toward the top of the tail. Remove the blanket from the sewing machine. Pin and stitch the other half. Once you have sewn both halves, you can try out the blanket. Check the seams and make sure you're happy with the stitching. Restitch any problem areas.

6 Fold the top of the tail over 1½˝ all the way around and press. Pin all the way around. **D**

7 Sew the hem (see Hemming Knit Fabric, page 15). You are sewing on the stretchy width of fabric, so take care not to pull it; otherwise you'll get a wavy edge. Just keep it flat and let it go through the machine. Stop when you are back to where you started and you've stitched over the beginning zigzags about 1˝. **E**

TIP ● *Your machine may get stuck when you sew over the side seams, with the thick, multiple layers of fabric. You can help the fabric go through the machine by gently pulling it out.*

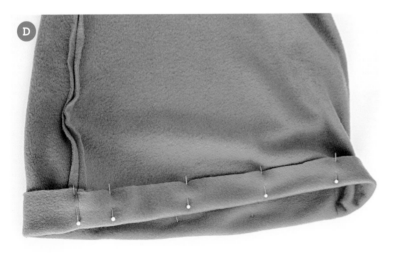

8 Trim the tips of the flippers to reduce the thickness so you can get a nice pointy shape when you turn them right side out. **F**

9 Turn the entire blanket right side out. Push out the flippers with a point turner, pencil, or chopstick, and shape it well by pressing with the iron. You are almost done!

10 To give the tail more shape and reinforce the bottom, topstitch all around the flipper. First, pin around the edge of the flipper. Set the machine to the largest straight stitch (length 5 on my machine) and topstitch with a ½˝ seam allowance. Start at the seam connecting the body and tail and continue around the flipper to seam's opposite side. **G**

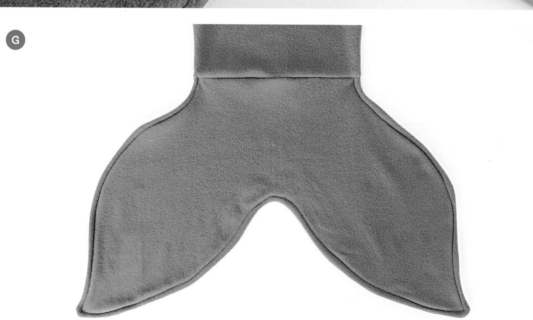

add the scales

Now you are free to design scales on the tail and have fun with colorful puffy paint or glitter. A glow-in-the-dark paint can be very cool too!

1 Trace your design with an erasable fabric-marking pen. (I think a FriXion pen works best; the ink disappears when you iron on it.) **H**

2 When you are happy with your design, go over the lines with puffy paint. (I used silver glitter puffy paint, but you could instead use glow-in-the-dark puffy paint that comes in various colors.) Let it dry overnight.

3 Make sure the paint is completely dry. Turn the mermaid tail wrong side out and iron on the wrong side only. Don't iron directly on the paint; otherwise it might melt and damage your project and the iron too.

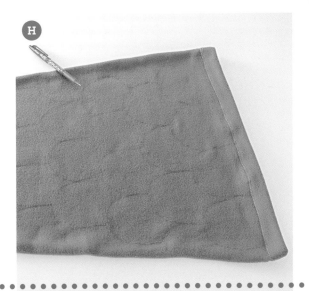

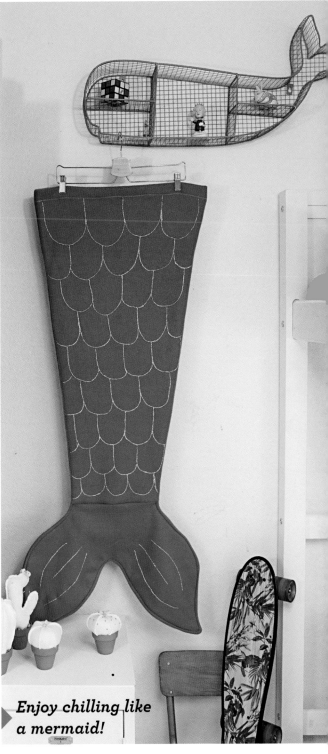

Enjoy chilling like a mermaid!

glow-in-the-dark light bulb

5½˝ wide × 8˝ high × 2˝ deep

This light bulb made of fabric will add a touch of fantasy to your room.

And it is not entirely fake.… Turn the light off and watch it glow in the dark!

- Unbleached cotton cloth or white cotton canvas, 1 scrap 7″ × 8″ for front

- Cotton print, 1 scrap 7″ × 8″ for bulb back

- Scraps for bulb top, front, and back

- Polyfill stuffing

- Chunky yarn, 2-yard length

- Glow-in-the-dark fabric paint (page 15)

- Puffy paint (page 12), black or another dark color

- Basic sewing kit (page 8)

⚠ Hot Tools (page 9)

- Iron

Pattern

- Download and print the Glow-in-the-Dark Light Bulb pattern. (See Downloading Patterns, page 25.)

prepare the pieces

1 Trace and cut 2 top pieces in assorted cotton.

2 Trace and cut 1 bulb in print cotton for the back.

3 Trace—*but do not cut*—1 bulb piece in cotton canvas for the front.

4 Paint the cotton canvas bulb that has not been cut out yet with a generous coat of glow-in-the-dark paint. Let it dry a few hours.

5 Tape the pattern to a window and place the painted bulb on top of it, facing you. Trace the filament with an erasable fabric-marking pen.

6 You have 2 options for creating the filament: You can go over it with puffy paint, and then let it dry overnight. Or if you are patient and love hand sewing, you can use a running stitch to make a pretty embroidered filament (see the modified running stitch used for the Dolman T-Shirt, page 63). When you are done, cut out around the shape.

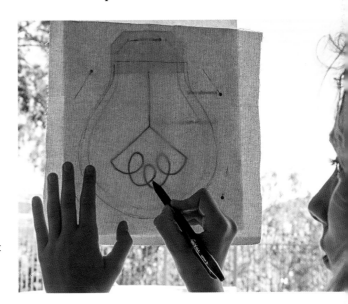

step by step

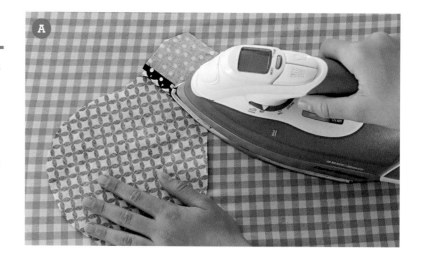

It's easy to make ⅜″–½″ seam allowances: Just line up the edge of a regular sewing foot with the edge of the fabric.

1 Pin the print top and print bulb fabric pieces right sides together. Sew them together. Repeat with the painted bulb and second print top.

2 Open the seams with the iron and press nicely on the wrong side. Don't press too long; otherwise you'll melt the paint. **A**

3 Pin the pieced bulbs right sides together. Mark the no-sew zone (page 18) on top of the bulb. You will need this gap to turn the bulb right side out, to stuff it, and to attach the yarn for hanging.

4 Start sewing at the beginning of the no-sew zone around to the opposite side. Backstitch at the beginning and end. **B**

5 Cut little snips in the curves to ease the fabric around the shape but be careful not to cut through the stitching. **C**

6 Turn the bulb inside out and push the curves and corners out to get a pretty bulb shape. Press on the print cotton side to remove the creasing.

7 Turn the edges of the no-sew zone to the inside and press to mark the seam. It will be helpful to have a nice crease where you'll need to hand stitch later.

8 Generously stuff the bulb with polyfill.

9 Knot one end of the 2-yard length of yarn. Insert the knotted end into the no-sew zone and center it. Pin in place.

10 Thread a needle with coordinating thread. Hand stitch along the no-sew zone, using a whipstitch (page 17), until you reach the yarn. Switch to a tiny running stitch (page 16) through the yarn, and then restart a whipstitch on the other side to finish the seam.

Now, you can hang your light!
There's no need to plug it in; it will brighten the dark wherever you put it!

couching stitch pillow 14″ × 6½″

May I have some help, please?

Make pillows that express sweet thoughts with words or phrases. The couching stitch is very easy and results in an outstanding finish that wows everyone. Perfect to personalize your room with, this decorative pillow can also be dedicated to someone you love. Stitch a name on and it becomes an adorable, unique gift!

- Unbleached cotton canvas, 1 square 15˝ × 15˝

- Cord, 1 yard (You can use any type of cord, but firm and not too thick or thin.)

- Coordinating thread, 2 colors (one to match cotton canvas, the other to match cord)

- Yarn for tassels

- Polyfill stuffing

- Fabric glue stick (washable)

- Basic sewing kit (page 8)

⚠ Hot Tools (page 9)

- Iron

Optional

- Large embroidery hoop, about 10˝ diameter

Patterns

- Download and print the Couching Stitch Pillow word pattern (*Create* or *Love*). (See Downloading Patterns, page 25.)

Another option: If you prefer, you could download and print a word (*hello, cool, relax, bonjour, happy,* or *sweet*) from the Dolman T-Shirt (page 63) or use your own word that fits in a 10˝ × 4˝ space.

prepare the pieces

1 Use the word you printed out or write your own word in cursive and tape it to a window.

2 Fold the 15˝ × 15˝ canvas square in half to get a center crease in both directions. Center the canvas over the word, both top to bottom and side to side. Once you have centered the canvas over the word, tape the canvas to the window as well.

3 Trace the word with a fabric-marking pen onto the canvas.

Now you are ready to use a couching stitch (page 60) on the fabric.

how to make the couching stitch

Couching means to attach a thick thread or cord to a background fabric by hand stitching. The term comes from the French word *coucher*, which means "to lay down."

Start by bringing the needle up from the back, about ¼˝ from beginning of the word. Put the needle back in on the opposite side of the cord, making a small vertical or slightly diagonal stitch.

Repeat along the cord at regular intervals. Stitches can be about a ¼˝ apart. You can increase this distance along straight lines and reduce it in the curves.

You'll certainly need 2 or 3 arm's lengths of thread to stitch a word. When you are finished stitching, about ¼˝ from the end of the cord, tie a double knot. Here's how: Take the needle to the back of the fabric. Make a secure knot by taking a small stitch on the back, making a small loop. Pull the thread through the loop to secure the stitch. Do this twice to tie a double knot.

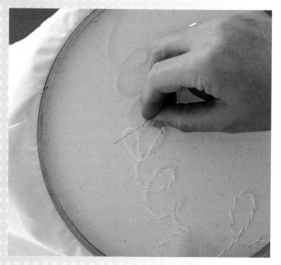

step by step

It's easy to make ⅜″–½″ seam allowances: Just line up the edge of a regular sewing foot with the edge of the fabric.

1 Lay the cord on the word you traced to roughly measure the length you need. Cut that length. Trace over the word with a fabric glue stick and attach the cord along the lines. **Ⓐ** Pin the cord in place where needed, especially where the lines are very curvy or where the cord overlaps. It will be very helpful at this point to have the canvas stretched onto an embroidery hoop (see Using an Embroidery Hoop, page 22).

2 Thread a needle with coordinating thread, measure an arm's length, and double it. Start sewing the cord to the fabric with a couching stitch (see How to Make the Couching Stitch, page 60) and remove the pins as you work.

3 When the word is totally stitched and you have tied a knot at the end, remove the canvas from the embroidery hoop. Press with an iron to remove any wrinkles and the marking pen lines. **Ⓑ**

4 Fold the square in half, right sides together, along the length of the word, and pin the raw edges together. Sew only the long edge of the fabric together, backstitching at the beginning and end. **Ⓒ**

5 Now you have a tube. Place the seam in the middle as shown in the photo. Press the seam open with an iron. **Ⓓ**

6 Make 4 tassels (see Making a Tassel, page 20).

TIP ● *Tassels will add a touch of whimsy to your pillow and are very easy to make. You can make them with yarn, embroidery floss, felt, or even T-shirt fabric strips!*

---

7 Place a tassel between the right sides of the pillow. Pin the tail of a tassel in each corner. Only the tails will be captured in the seam. Mark a 3″–4″ no-sew zone (page 18) on one side as an opening for turning and stuffing the pillow. **E**

8 Sew both short sides. Sew back and forth over the corners to secure the tassels.

9 To strengthen the tassels, tie a double knot with the tails of each tassel to make them more secure. **F**

10 Now gently turn the pillow right side out and give it a nice press with the iron. Now you get to stuff it with polyfill. **G**

11 Pin the opening and close it with a whip-stitch (page 17). **H**

● ▶ **Congratulations! Your pillow is done!**

Now you can create an assortment of pretty pillows like this with words and sayings!

Gallery

dolman t-shirt Youth sizes 8–16

Some experience required

Make a fancy personalized shirt and have fun with trims, lace, and pom-poms! Learn how to write on fabric with a simple running stitch to make a shirt that expresses your thoughts or motto. No doubt you'll get compliments! But shhh ... don't tell anyone how easy it was to make!

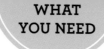
- T-shirt knit fabric (nonstretch), 58″ wide, 1 yard

- Embroidery floss or perle cotton thread

- Trims, 2-yard length of one kind or 18″ lengths of several kinds

- Lightweight fusible interfacing, 1 rectangle 10″ × 5″

- Fusible double-sided tape

- Jersey or ballpoint sewing machine needle

- Parchment paper for tracing the pattern

- Basic sewing kit (page 8)

⚠ Hot Tools (page 9)

- Iron

Optional

- Large embroidery hoop, about 10″ diameter

Patterns

- Use the Dolman T-Shirt front and back patterns (pullout page P3). Download and print a word pattern (*hello, cool, relax, bonjour, happy,* or *sweet*). (See Downloading Patterns, page 25.)

Another option: If you prefer, you could download and print a word pattern (*Create* or *Love*) from the Couching Stitch Pillow (page 58) or use your own word that fits in a 10″ × 4″ space.

prepare the pieces

1 Find your size by comparing your upper body measurements with the sizes in the Body Size Chart (page 22).

2 Trace the front and back pattern matching your size onto parchment paper. Using paper scissors, cut along the pencil line.

3 Your purchased fabric comes already folded along the grainline. If you have prewashed and dried the fabric, refold it the way it came (selvages matching) and press it with an iron.

4 To prepare the fabric for cutting, open the fold and bring the right and left selvages into the center crease. You will still have 2 layers of fabric, but there will be folds along both sides.

5 Place the pattern pieces on the fabric as shown in the cutting diagram (below). Pin the pattern and fabric together and cut out the pieces with fabric scissors.

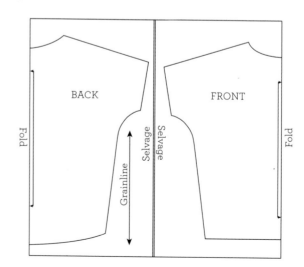

customizing your t-shirt

The Stitched Word

1 : Draw a line on the wrong side of the T-shirt front just under the curve of the armhole from side to side. Use an erasable fabric-marking pen or a chalk marker along with a flat ruler.

2 : Center the lightweight fusible interfacing on the wrong side of the shirt front with the sticky side (the textured one) down. Allow it to drop below the drawn line a little bit. Your word will be stitched through this piece of interfacing. Following the manufacturer's instructions, iron the interfacing in place. 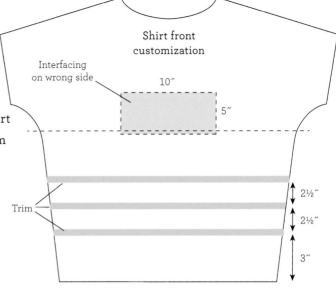 Ⓐ

3 : Turn the word over and lay it on top of the interfacing, centering it on the T-shirt side to side. Line up the bottom of the word with the line on the shirt. Pin in place.

4 : Flip the T-shirt over so it is right side up. With an erasable fabric-marking pen or a chalk marker, trace the word onto the shirt front. Tracing the line under the arm curve can help to write straight and stay in the frame of the interfacing placed on the opposite side.

5 : Insert the written area to stitch in an embroidery hoop, right side facing you. If the word doesn't fit in the hoop, put the hoop around the first part of the word and move it as you stitch (see Using an Embroidery Hoop, page 22). Ⓑ

Shirt front customization

Interfacing on wrong side

10˝

5˝

Trim

2½˝

2½˝

3˝

6 Hint: *Before you stitch, you can use an erasable pen to mark exactly where you will place the stitches. Be consistent, but adapt the size of the stitch as you go around shapes. Long, straight lines allow a long stitch and curves may force you to shorten the stitches.*

Thread a needle with embroidery floss or perle cotton. Stitch the embroidered word, using a modified version of the running stitch (page 16). Instead of using even stitching on the back and front of the fabric, make the stitch shorter on the back and longer on the front. The word will look nicer and be easier to read. **C**

7 Tie a knot close to the back of the fabric when you get to the end. Carefully iron your stitched word to remove the erasable pen markings. Don't forget to admire your work!

Sewing the Trims

1 Measure the width of the shirt front. Cut the trims 1˝ longer than the width of the shirt. Place the double-sided fusible tape on the back of each trim. Press with an iron to stick the tape to the trim, and then peel off the paper backing. **D**

2 Place the shirt front on the ironing board and position the trims as you like. Each trim should hang over the sides about ½˝. Use the shirt front customization diagram (page 65) as a guide. I placed the bottom trim 3˝ from the shirt's bottom edge, with 2½˝ spacing between each trim. But you can arrange them as you like.

3 Press the trims onto the shirt with the iron.

4 ⋮ Thread your machine with coordinating thread and set up for a narrow zigzag stitch that fits your lace trims. Sew close to the edge on top of the trims, one by one. If you chose pom-pom trim, use a zipper presser foot and a straight stitch (for help, see Chalkboard Backpack, Step by Step, Step 2, page 13). In general, you want to adapt your stitching to the kind of trim you are adding. **E**

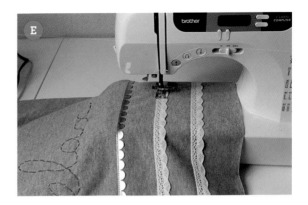

Yay! The customization is done!

Let's make the shirt! • ▶

step by step

It's easy to make ⅜˝–½˝ seam allowances: Just line up the edge of a regular sewing foot with the edge of the fabric.

1 ⋮ Place the shirt front and back right sides together and pin along the shoulders and the top of the sleeves. **F**

2 ⋮ Set up the sewing machine to do a straight stitch and sew along this edge. Backstitch at the beginning and end.

3 ⋮ Pin down the sides of the shirt from the edge of the sleeve to the bottom. Sew a straight stitch along this edge. Backstitch at the beginning and end. **G**

Cut the ends of the trims popping out on the wrong side of the shirt.

4 Now, if you consider the raw edges pretty, you are done! T-shirt knits don't fray a lot and raw edges make a kind of sporty look. **H**

5 If you want clean and neat edges, follow the instructions for Hemming Knit Fabric (page 15). **I**

Flip the shirt over and give it a nice press with an iron.

Try it out and let the shirt express your thoughts! • • •

skirt with shaped pockets

Youth sizes 8–16

Some experience required

*Because pockets make **all** the difference and even add a touch of whimsy! No need for a skirt pattern—just cut two identical rectangles to fit your measurements.*

- Denim or any cotton fabric, 44″ or wider, ½–¾ yard for skirt

- Solid color medium-weight cotton, 1 fat quarter for pockets

- ½″ flat knitted elastic for waistband

- Basic sewing kit (page 8)

⚠ Hot Tools (page 9)

- Iron

Patterns

- Download and print the Skirt with Shaped Pockets pattern for the pocket you want (cat, diamond, or heart). (See Downloading Patterns, page 25.)

  Another option: If you prefer, you could draw your own shape no larger than 7″ × 7″.

prepare the pieces

Skirt

1 For the skirt body, cut 2 rectangles from the denim or other skirt fabric. To find the size that fits you the best, take your measurements and fill in the blanks in the chart below.

Skirt Cutting Chart

To calculate	1. Write down your measurements.	2. Do a little math.	3. Write down each measurement total.
Width of skirt panels	Hips:	Add 10″; then divide by 2.	
Length of skirt panels	From waist to knee:	Add 3½″.	
Length of waist elastic	Waist:	Subtract 2″.	

For example: For a girl with 24˝ waist and 38˝ hips who wants a skirt length of 19˝, see the calculations in the sample chart below.

Sample Skirt Cutting Chart

To calculate	1. Write down your measurements.	2. Do a little math.	3. Write down each measurement total.
Width of skirt panels	Hips: **38˝**	Add 10˝; then divide by 2: **38˝ + 10˝ = 48˝** **48˝ ÷ 2 = 24˝**	**24˝**
Length of skirt panels	From waist to knee: **19˝**	Add 3½˝: **19˝ + 3½˝ = 22½˝**	**22½˝**
Length of waist elastic	Waist: **24˝**	Subtract 2˝: **24˝ – 2˝ = 22˝**	**22˝**

2 ⋮ To cut the rectangles, fold the fabric in half, right sides together (the way the fabric came when you bought it). Draw the rectangle on the wrong side of the fabric, with the length of skirt parallel to the fold. In the case of the sample skirt, the 22½˝ measurement would run along the fold. Cut through both layers.

3 ⋮ Cut the elastic to the length you calculated in the chart. By subtracting 2˝ from your waist measurement, the elastic will be just the right size to hold your skirt firmly above the hips.

4 ⋮ Cut 4 pockets from the medium-weight solid cotton.

step by step

It's easy to make ⅜˝–½˝ seam allowances: Just line up the edge of a regular sewing foot with the edge of the fabric.

Pockets

1 Place 2 pockets right sides together and pin in place.

2 Mark a 2˝ no-sew zone (page 18) for turning the pocket right side out. Make sure the no-sew zone is on the side of a pocket. See the patterns for suggested locations.

3 Starting at one end of the no-sew zone, sew around the edge of the pocket to the other side of the no-sew zone. Backstitch at the beginning and end.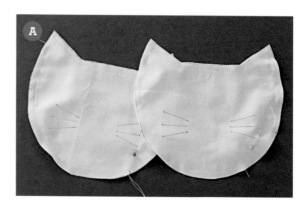

4 Prior to turning the pockets inside out, snip the curves and trim the corners. Turn inside out through the no-sew zone.

5 Push the corners out and give it a nice press with an iron. Fold in the seam allowances of the no-sew zone and press.

6 If you are making the diamond pocket, the cat, or another design that has extra details to be stitched, use an erasable pen to mark the stitching lines.

7 Thread the machine with a thread color that will enhance the pocket. Sew all the lines; backstitch lightly at the beginning and end of each line of stitching.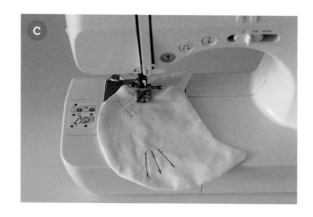

8 ┇ Now the pockets are ready to sew onto the skirt. Place the skirt front right side facing you. Place the pockets as shown on the placement diagram, centered on the front panel, 5˝ apart and 8˝ from the top. Pin in place. **D**

9 ┇ Topstitch close to the edge of each pocket, starting and ending on the marks shown on the placement diagram. Be sure to use a strong backstitch at the beginning and end so you can use the pockets. Topstitching over the no-sew zone will hold the seam allowances in place.

Skirt

1 ┇ Place the 2 skirt panels right sides together and pin the sides. Stitch the side seams with a straight stitch.

2 ┇ Sew along the raw edges of each seam with a narrow zigzag stitch. This will finish the edges nicely and prevent them from raveling. **E**

> **NOTE**
> **More about Pinning** *Placing the pins across the stitching line is another way to pin. For nonpile fabrics, such as cottons, that won't slip and distort, pinning like this makes removing the pins easy when you're at the sewing machine.*

3 ┇ Make a casing for the elastic waist. Fold the top edge of the skirt ½˝ to the wrong side and press. Fold in another 1½˝ and press again. Pin in place all the way around. Mark a 1˝ no-sew zone (page 18) at the back of the skirt for inserting the elastic. **F**

4 ┇ Starting at one end of the no-sew zone, sew around the inner edge of the fold to the other end of the no-sew zone. Backstitch at both ends.

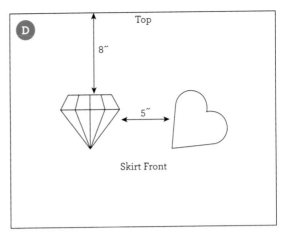

Pocket placement

5 Attach a safety pin to the end of the elastic to guide it through the casing. Attach the other end to the skirt at the casing opening with a pin, so it won't get pulled into the casing too far. **G**

6 Push the safety pin into the casing and work it through the channel. Push, push, and pull all the way around! Make sure the elastic stays flat and doesn't twist in the casing.

7 Remove the pins, overlap the ends of the elastic about 1˝, and repin. Use a large zigzag stitch to sew them together. **H**

8 Stretch out the elastic to distribute it all around the casing. Sew the opening you left with a straight stitch.

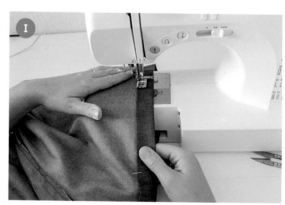

9 To hem the bottom of the skirt, see Hemming Cotton Fabric (page 35). **I**

Turn the skirt right side out and proudly slide your hands in the pockets! • • • • •

raglan sweatshirt

Youth sizes 8–16

Some experience required

The raglan sweatshirt is a must have in your wardrobe and a classic for the seamstress. Let's find out how to make it!

- Nonstretch sweatshirt-knit fabric or jersey knit with small stretch, 58˝ wide, 1⅔ yards

  Another option: Use fabric in 2 colors: ⅔ yard for body and 1 yard for sleeves.

- Scrap of fabric and fusible web 7˝ × 11˝, or just iron-on vinyl 7˝ × 11˝, for appliqué

- Jersey or ballpoint sewing machine needle

- Parchment paper for tracing

- Basic sewing kit (page 8)

⚠ Hot Tools (page 9)

- Iron

Patterns

- Use the Raglan Sweatshirt front, back, and sleeve patterns (pullout pages P2 and P4). Download and print the appliqué pattern (cactus, cat, or tree). (See Downloading Patterns, page 25.)

prepare the pieces

Raglan Sweatshirt

1 Find your size by comparing your upper body measurements with the sizes in the Body Size Chart (page 22).

2 Place parchment paper on top of the pattern and with a pencil, trace the front, back, and sleeve in the size you'll be making. Make sure to mark the notches (V-shaped marks on the raglan edges). Using paper scissors, cut along the pencil line.

3 Lay the fabric out flat, wrong side up, and then fold in the left selvage until you have a section the width of the back and front patterns. *Note: One pattern piece is upside down.* You may need to do this sometimes to fit the patterns onto the fabric. Pin the back and front patterns in place along the fold.

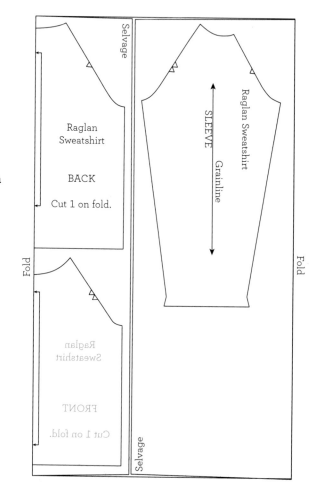

4 Fold the right selvage in to meet the left selvage to make another double-layer of fabric. Place the sleeve in this section, with the long edge of the sleeve aligned with the lengthwise grain.

5 Trace the around the patterns, remove them, and cut each piece out with fabric scissors.

6 If the fabric edges fray, stitch around all the cut edges with a regular zigzag stitch.

Front Embellishment

On the paper back of the fusible web, draw a shape in a size that fits your shirt and appliqué fabric. I drew a simple cactus, but you can use whatever design you like. To learn how to prepare, fuse, and stitch the shape to your sweatshirt front, see Fusible Appliqué (page 19). If you want, try an iron-on vinyl (see Tip, at right) for this project.

TIP ● Embellishing with iron-on vinyl: *Iron-on transfer sheets offer a variety of shimmery surfaces, vibrant colors, and trendy patterns. If you choose this option instead of fabric for your appliqué, see Iron-On Vinyl (page 14) for instructions.*

step by step

It's easy to make ⅜″–½″ seam allowances: Just line up the edge of a regular sewing foot with the edge of the fabric.

Raglan Sweatshirt

1 With the front sweatshirt panel facing you, place the sleeve right sides together. Match the notches of the sleeve to those on the front panel. Pin in place. Repeat with the other sleeve.

2 If you are using stretch fabric, sew each seam with a narrow zigzag (length 3 and width 1). Regular straight seams will break as the sweatshirt stretches! If you are using regular cotton fabric, you can use a straight stitch. Backstitch at the beginning and end.

3 : With the front panel and sleeves facing you pin the back panel, right sides together to the raglan sleeves, matching the notches. Stitch as you did in Step 2. **B**

4 : Pin front to back, right sides together, along the sides and down the sleeves, matching the underarm seams. **C**

5 : Stitch from the bottom edge of the sweatshirt to the underarm seam and down to the cuff of the sleeve. Repeat on the other side of the garment.

6 : Hem the bottom, neckline, and cuffs (see Hemming Knit Fabric, page 15). Turn the shirt right side out and give it a nice press. **D**

TIP ● *Take great care of your handmade clothes! Prior to washing them in the machine, don't forget to turn them inside out to protect the appliqué or vinyl pieces. Even better, wash them by hand or use a very gentle cycle! And make sure to hang dry rather than machine dry.*

Gallery

beanie hat

18˝–22˝ head size

Beginner-friendly

Beanie hats are so cute! Kids and grown-ups love them alike. The largest size might work for adults, too (check the size of your head). The pattern includes a kitty, bear, or basic beanie hat, but feel free to create other unique ear shapes!

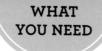
- Knit fleece or regular fleece fabric, 1 rectangle 18″ × 21″

- Basic sewing kit (page 8)

Optional

- Puffy paint (page 12)

Patterns

- Download and print the Beanie Hat pattern for the hat you want (beanie, kitty, or teddy bear). (See Downloading Patterns, page 25.)

finding your head size

This head size chart is just for your information; head sizes can vary widely. Use a tape measure around the widest part of the head, usually just above the ears, to find the pattern size that will fit you best, no matter what age you are.

Head Size Chart

Age	Head measurement	My head measurement
8–10	18″ (46 cm)	
12–14	20″ (51 cm)	
16 and up	22″ (56 cm)	

prepare the pieces

1 Using the Head Size Chart (above right), cut out the pattern you need for your head measurement.

2 Place the pattern on the fabric, aligning the bottom straight edge of the hat with the stretchy cross grain of the fabric. (You may have to test the fabric to see which way stretches the most.) Trace the pattern onto the fleece with a fabric pen. If a fabric pen doesn't work on fleece, try a chalk marker.

3 You can cut out the back and front separately or double the fabric and cut them together. If you cut them together, pin the ears and skip over the dart (the little V on top of the hat). Cut the darts out one at a time, because it's really difficult to cut them out two at a time.

step by step

It's easy to make ⅜″–½″ seam allowances: Just line up the edge of a regular sewing foot with the edge of the fabric.

1 : Fold each piece in half, right sides together, and pin the dart. Sew the dart seam together using a straight stitch. You will start at the top of the hat and sew off the folded edge back-stitching at both ends. **A**

2 : Place the front and back pieces right sides together. Pin only the right half of the hat together from top to bottom. **B**

TIP ● *Because the fabric is stretchy, it is best to sew section by section from top to bottom to prevent the edge from distorting while sewing. If you sew all the way around from bottom to bottom, the two layers can easily shift. You will continue to use a straight stitch here.*

3 : On the side you pinned, sew from the top center of the hat toward the bottom. Gradually reduce the seam allowance to ¼″ around the ears. Pivot cleanly at the tips of the kitty ears or stitch a nice curve for the teddy bear ears.

TIP ● *Since you are starting to sew at the bumpy dart, you can help the machine by pulling out the threads behind the needle and gently holding them as you begin to sew.* **C**

4 : Repeat Steps 2 and 3 for the other side of the hat. **D**

NOTE Fraying *Usually, fleece fabrics don't fray. But if you notice raw edges fraying in your hat, just resew each seam with a narrow zigzag stitch covering the raw edge; this will finish the seam and prevent the edges from fraying.*

5 Now you just need to hem the bottom. Try on the hat to determine how much you want to turn inside. The hem may be around 1″, but make it as deep or narrow as you like (see Hemming Knit Fabric, page 15).

6 Feel free to add cute whiskers with paint, a pom-pom, or whatever else you wish to give life to your hat!

Look to the gallery for inspiration!

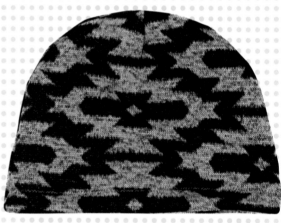

hand-printed apron

Some experience required

An apron for cooking, crafting, painting, gardening ... whatever you like! This apron is so pretty that you'll find a lot of reasons to wear it! Made from unbleached cloth, the fabric is like a blank page where you can experiment with different decorative techniques. Have fun designing, painting, and stenciling!

- Unbleached cotton cloth (canvas), 1 yard for apron

- Muslin, 1 yard for apron lining

- Cotton print, ½ yard for pocket and ties

- Parchment for tracing

- Basic sewing kit (page 8)

⚠ Hot Tools (page 9)

- Iron

For doily stenciling

- Paper doilies, 5˝–10˝

- Fabric paint

- Sponge brush for stenciling

- Quilt batting spray

Pattern

- Copy or trace the Hand-Printed Apron's armhole cutting guide (pullout page P1).

prepare the pieces

1 ⋮ Cut a canvas rectangle 20˝ × 24½˝. Trim the Armhole Cutting Guide along the outside line. Place it across the right top corner of the canvas rectangle and use an erasable fabric-marking pen to trace the armhole. Copy the placement marks for the ties. Turn the pattern over and align it with the top left corner of the canvas rectangle to mark the other armhole and tie placements. Cut the armholes with the fabric scissors.

2 ⋮ Cut a rectangle 20˝ × 24½˝ from the muslin and use the canvas front as a pattern to cut out the lining.

3 ⋮ Cut ties for the neck and waist from the print fabric only. Do this first before cutting the pocket from the same fabric. Cut 1 tie 3˝ × 35˝ for the waist and 1 tie 3˝ × 24˝ for the neck.

4 ⋮ For the pocket, use a ruler and erasable fabric-marking pen to draw an 11˝ × 8˝ rectangle on the wrong side of the print fabric; cut. Cut out another pocket from the muslin lining.

TIP ● *You can use a sheet of letter-size paper as a pattern for the front pocket; the paper is only ½˝ larger than the front pocket.*

Stenciling with Doilies

1 ⋮ Get ready for painting. Protect your clothes by wearing an oversize shirt or painting smock. Protect your worktable by covering it with newspaper or craft paper. This way you won't get adhesive spray or paint on the table. Place a doily on the protected area of the table. If the doily is wrinkled, press it first with the iron on medium heat. Barely spray some adhesive on one side—just a little bit. **A**

2: Carefully pick up the doily and place the sticky side on the apron where you want to stencil. With your hands, press down well to make sure it stays in place. You don't want it to move while you are painting and you don't want the paint to bleed underneath the stencil.

3: Using the sponge stenciling brush, apply the paint by tapping up and down all over the doily. Do not brush sideways; otherwise you might rip the doily or cause paint to seep through. **B**

4: Remove the doily carefully. **C**

5: Repeat with more doily designs, if you wish. If you want the designs to overlap on top of each other, let the first doily's paint dry before starting the next one. **D**

6: Let the paint dry overnight, then iron the design with a pressing cloth or pressing sheet. Both of these protect the design and the iron while heat setting the paint. This makes the design more permanent. Pressing cloths and sheets are heat resistant and can be found at most craft or fabric stores.

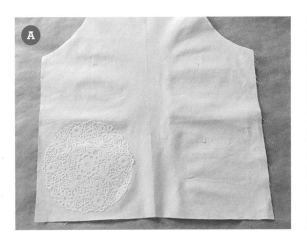

step by step

It's easy to make ⅜˝–½˝ seam allowances: Just line up the edge of a regular sewing foot with the edge of the fabric.

Front Pocket

1 Place the pocket and its muslin lining right sides together and pin all the way around.

2 Mark a 2˝ no-sew zone on a short side for turning the pocket right side out. **A**

3 Starting at one side of the no-sew zone, sew all around the pocket to the opposite side, backstitching at the beginning and end and pivoting at the corners to change direction. Trim the corners on the diagonal to reduce bulk. **B**

4 Turn the pocket inside out through the no-sew zone. Use a stick to help push the corners out. Give it a nice press with an iron and make sure you have the edge of the no-sew zone properly folded to the inside (the gap should be barely visible). **C**

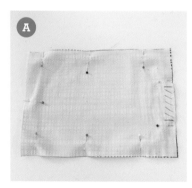

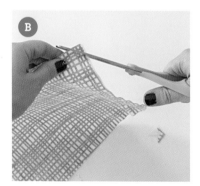

Ties for the Waist and Neck

1 Fold the 35˝ tie in half lengthwise, wrong sides together. Press with an iron to set a crease.

2 Open it up and fold the raw edges of both short ends in ½˝. Press. **D**

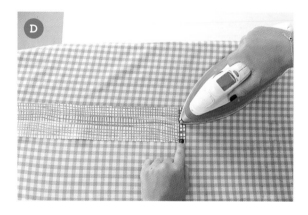

3: Fold and press the long edges to the center, using the center crease as a guide. **E**

4: Refold at the center crease so you have a long, skinny strip with folded edges. Press again and pin along the length.

5: Repeat with the 24″ tie, except fold *only one* short end over, not both. **F**

6: Use a straight stitch on your machine to topstitch very close to the edges on both long sides of each tie. **G**

7: Cut the ties to create the belt and the neck strap. **H**

- Cut the longer tie in half.

- Cut a 5″ long piece from the raw end of the short tie.

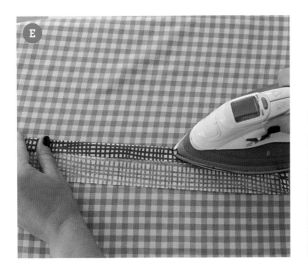

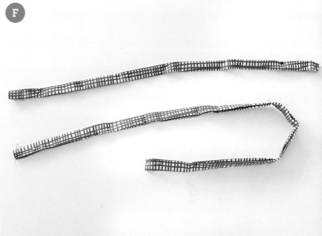

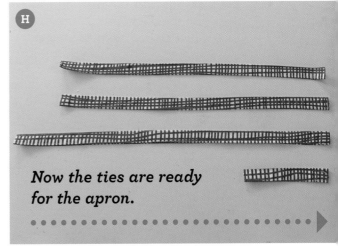

Now the ties are ready for the apron.

The Apron

1 Center the front pocket right side facing on the front of the apron, about 14½″ from the top of the apron. An easy way to center the pocket is by folding it and the apron in half vertically, then matching the folds. There should be 5″ from the side of the pocket to the side of the apron. Pin in place. If the printed pocket has a direction—a pattern you want to see right side up, for example—make sure it is placed properly. **A**

2 Topstitch around the sides and bottom of the pocket only, close to the edge. Backstitch at the beginning and end. You can sew an extra line down the middle of the pocket vertically (or divide it into a ⅔ / ⅓ split) to make a double pocket. **B**

3 Place the front apron panel in front of you and position the waist ties and neckties on their marks. **C**

WAIST   Place the raw end of each 17″ tie on the marks shown on the pattern, leaving ¼″ hanging past the edge of the apron.

NECK   Fold the 5″ short tie in half to make a loop and pin the raw edges on the mark at the neckline. Place the remaining tie on the other mark at the neckline, with ¼″ of the raw edge hanging past the edge of the apron.

Lay the rest of the ties' length over the apron front to prevent it from getting caught in any seam allowances. You want only the raw ends sewn into the seams.

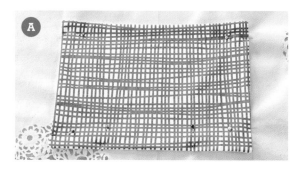

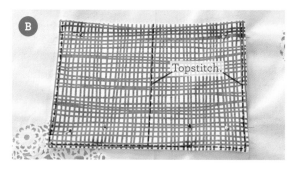

Topstitch.

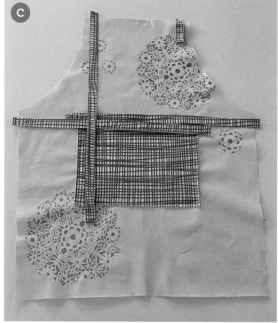

4 ⫶ Place the apron lining facedown on top of the front, aligning the raw edges. Pin from a bottom corner up and around to the other bottom corner, unpinning the neck loop on the way and repinning it to include the muslin lining. Keep the bottom edge open. **C**

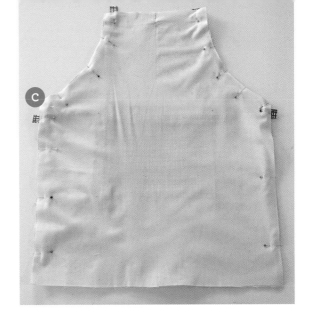

5 ⫶ Sew all the way around. Backstitch at the beginning and the end.

6 ⫶ Make little snips on the curves and trim the corners diagonally to help ease the fabric. **D**

7 ⫶ Turn the apron right side out through the bottom opening. With your hands, press it flat and pretty as you nudge the corners and curves out. Give it a nice press with the iron.

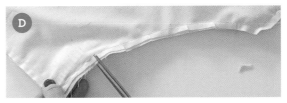

8 ⫶ Hem the bottom by folding the bottom edges ½˝ to the inside of the apron. Pin the folds together. Topstitch the hem closed. Keep topstitching all the way around the apron. This top stitch will provide a nice shape to the apron and make the ties stronger. **E**

You'll definitely be the best dressed for any crafting, painting, or baking project!

clear window zippy pouch 9½″ × 7½″

Clear vinyl offers so many possibilities for sewing projects! And when it's combined with nice fabrics and cute prints, it's even better. Stuff the front window with souvenirs, glitter, or sequins, and your zippy pouch will be the fanciest one of all!

Some experience required

- Heavyweight cotton,
  1 rectangle 11″ × 8½″ for back
  ··· and ···
  Medium-weight cotton print,
  1 rectangle 11″ × 8½″ for lining (*Note: The lining will be visible through the clear vinyl.*)

  Another option: Use 2 rectangles 11″ × 8½″ of heavyweight cotton for back and lining.

- Clear vinyl, 1 rectangle 11″ × 8½″ for front

- Zipper, 11″ length

- Matching cord, 7″ length
  (to attach to zipper pull)

- Zipper presser foot

- Small binder clips

- 1 sheet 8½″ × 11″ paper as a pattern

- Tiny special items to fill the clear window pouch, such as glitter, little toys, tiny gems, seashells …
  (*Note: Don't select anything organic that could mold or anything sharp that could rip the plastic!*)

- Basic sewing kit (page 8)

prepare the pieces

1 Use the sheet of paper as a pattern. The 8½″ edges will be the sides, and the 11″ edges will be top and bottom of the pouch. Place the pattern on the heavyweight cotton, short edge along the grainline. Trace and cut.

2 For the lining, repeat with the same fabric or a medium-weight cotton print, which will be visible through the clear vinyl.

3 To trace and cut the vinyl, lay the heavyweight cotton piece on the table and place the vinyl on top. Tape the vinyl to the table. With a ruler and a marker, trace the rectangle onto the vinyl. Cut with craft scissors.

step by step

It's easy to make ⅜˝–½˝ seam allowances: Just line up the edge of a regular sewing foot with the edge of the fabric.

1 Place the vinyl on the right side of the lining. With the right side of the zipper (zipper teeth popping up) facing the vinyl, align the zipper tape to the top edge of the vinyl. Attach these 3 layers with binder clips. Don't use pins; it's too thick and you don't want to puncture the vinyl. **A**

2 Attach a zipper presser foot to the sewing machine. Position it to fall to the right of the zipper on the zipper tape. Move the needle as far to the left as possible so that it will pass freely through the left hole of the presser foot but not so far left that the needle will break on the zipper coils. Also, stitching too close to the zipper teeth can prevent the slider from moving smoothly over the zipper.

3 Sew a straight line next to the zipper teeth, pulling the binder clips off as you sew. Backstitch at the beginning and end of the stitching. **B**

TIP ● You will need to move the zipper slider out of the way as you sew. Start the stitching with a closed zipper. As you approach the slider, secure the needle position by dropping the machine's needle down. Then lift the presser foot to move the zipper slider past the needle to the side you've already sewn. Finish the stitching.

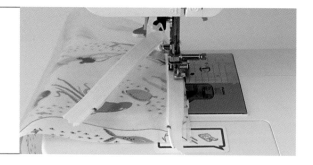

4 Open the seam and fold the layers away from the zipper. You can feel the rigidity of the vinyl. To keep it flat and pretty, finger-press the vinyl at the seamline. Use a nonstick presser foot and a large straight stitch to topstitch through all layers along the zipper. (*Note: If you don't have a nonstick pressure foot, you can just use a piece of washi tape on a regular presser foot; see Nonstick Presser Foot, page 9.*) **C**

5 Align the heavyweight cotton back, right sides together to the other side of the zipper. No need for paper clips this time—you can pin fabric and zipper together or use double-sided fusible tape, like I did in the Critter Coin Pouch (page 31). **D**

6 Repeat Step 3 to attach the zipper to the back. Topstitching the back to the zipper is optional.

7 Turn the pouch to the right side and move the zipper slider to the halfway point. Fold the pouch in half at the zipper, matching the front and back rectangles, right sides together. Pin from the zipper down each side and along the bottom of the pouch where you will leave a 3″ no-sew zone (page 18). You will need this gap to fill the vinyl window with the embellishments. **E**

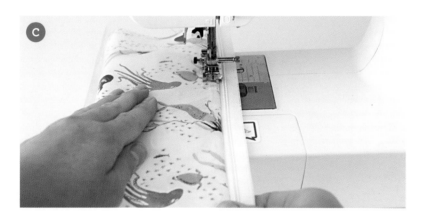

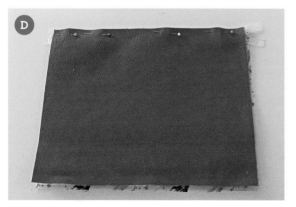

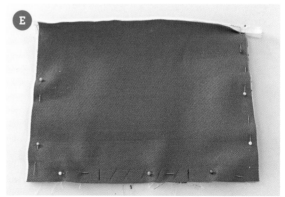

8 : Sew across the folded zipper and down the sides; pivot at the corner and stitch up to the no-sew zone. Backstitch at the beginning and end of the stitching, and repeat on the other side of the pouch.

9 : Pour some glitter or any other embellishment you would like into the pouch between the clear vinyl and the lining. Make sure you are using the right layers—not the back and the lining by mistake—otherwise you would be pouring embellishments on the floor! Do not overfill the space. **F**

10 : Once the pouch is filled, go back to the machine and stitch the no-sew zone closed, completing the bottom seam. Finish the 3 sides of the pouch by zigzagging along the raw edges. This will prevent fraying.

11 : Turn the pouch right side out through the zipper and push the corners out. It's not as easy as it was with past projects because of the rigidity of the vinyl.

Optional: Attach a cute piece of string or tassel to the zipper pull.

F

You are done! ●●●●●●●●●●●●●●●●● ▶
Check it out and see how pretty the embellishments look through the window!

Gallery

About the Author

A native of France and expatriate in the United States, Jennifer runs Little Print Fabrics Studio in San Diego, California, where kids and grown-ups love to come and sew creatively.

When Jennifer arrived in the United States with her three little girls and a very old 220V sewing machine, she was amazed by all the sewing and craft supplies that were readily available in her newly adopted country. She couldn't wait to sew for her new home and family.

She sewed as she never sewed before, and she started sharing her sewing journey through her blog, *My Little Print Fabrics*. She quickly had the opportunity to teach craft and sewing classes in local schools and was happy to discover a new generation of very creative girls eager to learn. Teaching others how to sew appeared to be a new vocation for Jennifer. Constantly inspired by her three daughters, Jennifer designed unique patterns for young sewists along the way, a hobby that quickly turned into a full-time career.

Besides her teaching commitments and an intensive schedule filled with learning and designing in her studio, Jennifer wanted to write a book that reflected the activities in her classes. As an enthusiastic lover of handmade textiles, unique personal accessories, and customized clothing, Jennifer wanted to create a book that would empower and encourage makers to personalize their projects in their own artistic fashion. This book answers the challenge of how to mix creativity and playful imagination with technical sewing skills successfully.

Photo by Olivier Colin

VISIT JENNIFER ONLINE!

Blog: mylittleprintfabrics.com

Instagram: @littleprintfabrics_studio

Facebook: /mylittleprintfabricsstudio

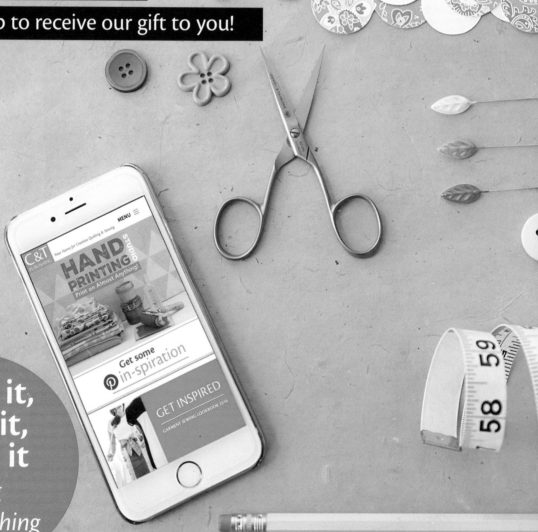

Want even more creative content?

Make it,
snap it,
share it
using
#ctpublishing